JEREMY LIN

JEREMY LIN

THE INCREDIBLE RISE OF THE NBA'S MOST UNLIKELY SUPERSTAR

BILL GUTMAN

SPORTS
PUBLISHING

Sports Publishing books may be purchased in bulk at special discounts for sales promotion, corporate gifts, fund-raising, or educational purposes. Special editions can also be created to specifications. For details, contact the Special Sales Department, Sports Publishing, 307 West 36th Street, 11th Floor, New York, NY 10018 or sportspubbooks@skyhorsepublishing.com.

Sports Publishing® is a registered trademark of Skyhorse Publishing, Inc.®, a Delaware corporation.

Visit our website at www.sportspubbooks.com

10 9 8 7 6 5 4 3 2 1

Library of Congress Cataloging-in-Publication Data
Gutman, Bill.
Jeremy Lin : the incredible rise of the NBA's most unlikely superstar / Bill Gutman.
p. cm.
ISBN 978-1-61321-278-3 (pbk. : alk. paper)
1. Lin, Jeremy, 1988 2. Basketball players—United States—Biography.
I. Title.
GV884.L586G87 2012
796.323092--dc23
[B]
2012025092

Printed in the United States of America

To my very good friends,
Thomas and Betty Jones

Contents

Introduction

WHAT ARE THE odds of a guy, sitting at the end of an NBA bench on the verge of being cut, being summoned into a game and suddenly starring in it? Okay, let's say that can happen. Most any athlete can suddenly find lightening in a bottle on a given night, but what if that same player earns a start because of the combination of that one game and several injuries to other players? What are the odds that he will not only take over the team from the demanding position of point guard, but lead a floundering, sub-.500 ballclub to an unlikely seven-game winning streak while breaking several longstanding records along the way? And then, what are the odds of that player, one of the very few Asian Americans to ever play in the NBA, not only becoming the toast of the town and the toast of the NBA, but the hottest commodity in all of sports?

It sounds like a pure fairytale; the ultimate underdog story—one that might be hard to believe if it were introduced as a piece of fiction—but it did happen . . . and to widespread fanfare. The point guard is Jeremy Lin of the New York Knicks, a player not recruited out of high school, a Harvard graduate not drafted by any NBA team, and a guy who was waived by two teams and almost cut by a third. Given a chance by Coach

Mike D'Antoni, whose Knicks team was a moribund 8-15 at the time, Lin showed both basketball and leadership skills that no one in the NBA knew he had. With the team's two resident stars, Carmelo Anthony and Amar'e Stoudemire, both out of the lineup, Lin fearlessly took control of the basketball and the ballclub, almost immediately making a group of players into a team and reviving one of the NBA's flagship franchises—one that had been on life support for years. The phenomenon of Linsanity was born.

Here's a quick look at the numbers. Through his first twenty-three games on the Knicks' bench to start the 2011–2012 season, Jeremy Lin played a total of fifty-five minutes. Then, on February 4, he came off the bench against the New Jersey Nets to score 25 points, while adding five rebounds and seven assists to lead the Knicks to a 99-92 victory. Given a start against the Utah Jazz (after his big night against New Jersey), he promptly showed that the first game wasn't a fluke, scoring 28 points and adding eight assists as the Knicks won again. Two days later, against the Washington Wizards, it was 23 points and 10 assists. Then he really exploded, scoring 38 points with seven assists as the Knicks beat Kobe Bryant and the Los Angeles Lakers. The story was becoming more improbable by the day. With the media beginning to swarm, people were taking notice and wondering just who Jeremy Lin really was.

Not only did Lin have the Knicks winning and Madison Square Garden jumping again, but he was achieving something that hadn't been seen in a long time. His 89, 109, and 136 total points after his first three, four, and five career starts, respectively, represented the most by any player since the

NBA/ABA merger in 1976–1977. He also became the first NBA player to score at least 20 points and add seven or more assists in each of his first four starts. After his fourth start, and the team's fifth-straight win, he was named the Eastern Conference Player of the Week, which he promptly followed by hitting a game-winning three-pointer against the Toronto Raptors with less than a second remaining on the clock, and bringing his team back from a 17-point deficit. When he had a career-high 13 assists in the next game against the Sacramento Kings, the Knicks had won seven straight and were back to .500 with a record of 15-15. By that time, everybody in the sporting world wanted to know more about Jeremy Lin and how his obvious talent could have gone unnoticed for so long.

But that still wasn't all. A confluence of circumstances had led to the widespread Linsanity that was, by now, sweeping the NBA and crossing over into other areas of the sports and sociological worlds. Before Jeremy Lin got his chance, the Knicks were again not winning, and Madison Square Garden, long known as the Mecca of Basketball, lacked any form of life. Fans still came out, but their expectations were definitely not high—at least not until Mike D'Antoni put the basketball in Jeremy Lin's hands. Suddenly, the Garden was again the place to be with loud, boisterous crowds and a gaggle of celebrities watching and socializing at each game. The print and broadcast media could not get enough of the story, and those in the know said that Lin's play had not only kept him from being cut, but he may very well have saved Coach D'Antoni's job for the moment. For sheer drama complete with media coverage, it couldn't have happened in a better place than New York.

In addition, the timing of Lin's arrival couldn't have been better for the entire league. Prior to the start of the season, the NBA owners had locked out the players over a protracted attempt to get a new agreement between themselves and the Players Association. The league, which had just come off a successful 2010–2011 campaign, suddenly had to deal with a never-ending spate of negative publicity. Fans viewed both the players and owners as greedy millionaires (and in some owners cases, billionaires) who were trying to squeeze the last dollar from each other. Negotiations were contentious and often downright mean-spirited. When the lockout was finally lifted and a new agreement was put in place, the league had to put together a compressed, 66-game schedule. There was much grumbling among the players, a rash of injuries due to the limited practice time, and star players looking to be traded to bigger markets à la LeBron James, who had moved from Cleveland to Miami the season before. It was the rise of Jeremy Lin that made the NBA alive and once again relevant in what, to that time, had been a mostly desultory season.

Throughout the Lin-led Knicks win streak, more and more information began to emerge about the 6'3" point guard out of Harvard who had been unceremoniously cut by both the Golden State Warriors and Houston Rockets in short order before he was claimed by the Knicks, essentially signed to just be another warm body at the end of the bench until a couple of players returned from injury. In fact, shortly before his unexpected emergence, he had been sent down to the Erie Bay Hawks of the NBA's D-League—a kind of minor league for players still not quite good enough for the NBA.

What made Lin's story more interesting and, ultimately, so marketable was his ethnicity. His parents had come to the United States from Taiwan and, while he was born in California, his Asian American heritage made him a source of pride in many Asian countries, including China—a prime target of the NBA's worldwide marketing effort. Ivy League graduates in the NBA were already a rare enough commodity, but Asian Americans were even rarer, giving more grist to the marketing and publicity mills. Also, his name lent itself to various puns, beginning with *Linsanity*. If the Knicks won and he had a big game, it was *Lincredible*. If he did something last second, it might be *Just Lin Time*. And that's just a brief sampling.

There was also an underside to the story: racial stereotyping where even several prominent journalists had to apologize for remarks they may have thought cute or funny, but actually played into anti-Asian bias. An ESPN writer was fired for coining a headline that read "Chink in the Armor" after a Knicks loss. It may be an old expression in which *chink* means a dent or blemish, but it's also a word that is extremely offensive to Asians and Asian Americans. Yet through it all, Jeremy Lin has prevailed, and the public has learned that he is a humble, self-effacing, and deeply religious young man who calls his sudden ascendency to fame and success a "Miracle of God."

Lin and the Knicks faced another period of adjustments when stars Amar'e Stoudemire and Carmelo Anthony returned to the team, along with several other new players, including J. R. Smith. But Coach D'Antoni indicated that the ball would remain in Jeremy's hands, and Lin himself quickly expressed optimism that the team would adjust and continue to win.

There was a great deal of pressure on Lin's slim shoulders, but he appeared ready for the challenge. As Kobe Bryant said when someone mentioned that Lin had seemingly come out of nowhere to score thirty-eight against the Lakers, "Players playing that well don't usually come out of nowhere. It seems like they come out of nowhere, but if you can go back and take a look, his skill level was probably there from the beginning. It probably just went unnoticed."

Jeremy's Lin's magical first season would take a couple of more U-turns before it ended prematurely. After Stoudemire and Anthony returned from injury, the teams began to flounder once again, losing all the magic that Lin's arrival had brought. Anthony in particular was having trouble functioning in D'Antoni's fast-paced, ball-movement offense. The result was inevitable. D'Antoni suddenly resigned, and his top assistant, former Atlanta Hawks head coach Mike Woodson, took over the team.

Woodson initially indicated that he might take the ball out of Jeremy's hands and hand the team over to veteran point guard Baron Davis, but Lin's grittiness and clutch play won him over, and he admitted that Lin was an integral part of the team, naming him the starting point guard for the remainder of the season. Unfortunately, a knee injury intervened. Jeremy first reported a sore knee and was expected to miss just a couple of games. A short time later, an MRI revealed a partial tear of the meniscus, and he opted for arthroscopic surgery, hoping to return if the Knicks could get past the first round of the playoffs. So the drama and the Lin countdown continued.

But before all the details on how the season played out, it's important to learn exactly how Jeremy Lin found his way from Palo Alto, California, to Harvard, then the NBA, and finally to having the ball in his hands at Madison Square Garden . . . as well as the sudden fame and popularity that contributed to him having the fastest selling jersey in the entire league.

Chapter One: The Road to Harvard

THOUGH JEREMY SHU-HOW Lin was born in Los Angeles on August 23, 1988, his family history goes back hundreds of years. His father, Gie-Ming Lin, and his mother, Shirley, came to the United States from Taiwan in the mid-1970s. Like so many others, they came to further their educations and hopefully carve out a better life for themselves and their family. They settled in Southern California, eventually moving to Palo Alto, where they raised three sons—Josh, Jeremy, and Joseph. Here's a quick look at their family history.

Mr. Lin's ancestors immigrated to Taiwan from Zhangpu County, Fujian, in mainland China in 1707. They were part of a mass migration from Fujian, and it is from these people that most of today's Taiwanese are descended. Though, in a strict sense, they are all Chinese, those who went to Taiwan consider themselves Taiwanese. The Lin family eventually settled in Beidou, Changhua, in Taiwan, and Mrs. Lin's maternal grandmother came to Southern Taiwan from Pinghu, Zhejiang, China in the late 1940s.

Because both his parents worked, Jeremy's grandmother, Lin Chu A Muen, came to California to help look after him when he was a young child, often feeding him traditional Taiwanese dishes, such as fried rice with dried turnips and eggs. She said he was always a mild-mannered young boy who didn't hesitate to share his possessions with his brothers and friends, showing all the characteristics of a future point guard.

Not surprisingly, basketball began early in Jeremy's life, thanks to his father falling in love with the game and teaching its finer points to his three boys. His father still plays the game and also collects basketball DVDs. As Lin Chu, Jeremy's grandmother, remembers, "My son, when he came home from work, would always take the kids to play basketball. He took Jeremy to the basketball courts as soon as he could walk."

Mr. Lin and the boys would go to the local YMCA where he would teach them the right way to play the game. They went nearly every evening, but there was one hard and fast rule that the three boys had to always follow. They couldn't go until all their homework was done. No exceptions.

From the beginning, studies always came first, and all three of the Lin children were diligent about their schoolwork, always bringing home good grades. Older brother, Josh, is presently a dental student at New York University, while younger brother, Joseph, is a student and basketball player at Hamilton College in Clinton, New York. As for Jeremy, it was felt that he would excel at academics, with any basketball success being a surprising bonus, as he was not expected to be very tall.

Both his parents were just 5'6", and when Jeremy started his freshman year at Palo Alto High School in 2002, he was just 5'3" and appeared to be on track to be about the same height as his mom and dad. What happened next is very reminiscent of the great Michael Jordan. No male member of the Jordan family was taller than 5'9", yet the great MJ wound up at 6'6". Someone once said that Jordan, who already loved basketball and wanted to be great, actually willed himself to become tall. Whether Jeremy Lin willed it or not, he surprised everyone by eventually growing a foot taller to his present height of 6'3".

"Luckily, I grew," Jeremy says now, looking back. "Maybe I was meant to be a basketball player."

But it didn't happen overnight. He was practicing constantly, at first with his brothers, and then finding pick-up games wherever he could.

"Anyplace we could find a hoop and a ball, we would play," he recalled. He remembers after attending their Friday night youth group meetings at the Chinese Church of Christ, the brothers would go directly to a gym at Stanford to play pick-up games and often stayed out until after 2:00 AM. That certainly befits the definition of a "gym rat," an expression often used to describe a guy who can't get enough of the game.

It was at the Jane Lathrop Stanford Middle School in Palo Alto where Jeremy began to make his mark on the court. Rick Chandler was running the tryouts for all the seventh and eighth graders and remembers what the school's athletic director, Mike Ferolino, told him.

"He said, 'There's this kid, Jeremy Lin,'" Chandler recalls, "'and you're not going to have to watch him very much. He's about the best player we've ever had here. He's going right to the A team.'"

But Lin didn't make an immediate impression on Chandler. "I don't think he said a single word during the week of tryouts,"

Chandler said. "But eventually his game came into focus and he was doing things eighth graders aren't supposed to be able to do. He saw everything two moves ahead, something rare for middle schoolers who, by nature, live in the moment. But Lin and his teammates, who had been playing together for two years, seemed to communicate by sonar.

"Toward the end of the first day, when Lin whipped a behind-the-back pass toward open air—only to have a team-mate appear at the last second to catch it and take two steps for a lay in—I had seen enough. My recommendation was to seal this kid in Bubble Wrap and store him in a cool, dry place until his freshman year of high school. No sense scuffing him up at this level."

Jeremy continued to play as often as he could and always with his parents' blessing, but with the caveat that he kept his grades up. If he had so much as an A-, his mom Shirley would warn him that basketball would be out unless he brought that grade up to an A. Yet she was always at his games and perhaps his biggest fan. During his high school years, she would organize rides to the games, book the hotel reservations for the family, and even print out statistics of upcoming opponents. She did all this while holding down a full-time job at Sun Microsystems, where she worked as an engineer for the computer science company.

Pete Diepenbrock, who would coach Jeremy at Palo Alto High, saw just how important Mrs. Lin was to her son. "You know how parents tell their kids they can do anything?" Diepenbrock said. "Most people just say it to say it, but Jeremy's mom *lives* it. Because of that, Jeremy's always had this ridiculous confidence level."

Before he reached high school, Jeremy played AAU ball in the summers; his team coached by a man named Jim Sutter. Coach Sutter soon noticed something that Jeremy's coaches would see all the way up the line.

"There are guys that are terrific players, but when the stage gets big, they shrink," Sutter said. "For Jeremy, it's always been that he glows—just glows—when he's in the spotlight. It's just his makeup. It's his determination to succeed."

Jeremy of course had to grow into his role at Palo Alto. He started out at 5'3", but continued to grow right through his senior year . . . and as he grew, his skill level also continued to grow. By his junior year at Palo Alto, he was the team's point guard and perhaps their best player. Palo Alto was surprising a lot of people, and some thought they had a chance to win the Northern California championship. Then, just before the finals, Jeremy severely injured his right ankle and had to sit as Palo Alto lost to the eventual champion, North Ridge. But the next year was a different story, as his ankle injury made him change his overall basketball perspective.

"I broke my ankle the night before the championship game," he recalled, later. "That changed my whole life because, before that, up to that point, I was a really bad practice player. I had a lot of attitude. I'd be kicked out of practice—just wouldn't listen to any of the coaches because I felt like I was the best player. But, once I broke my ankle, it changed my whole outlook. About everything. I just told myself, 'I don't know how long I'm going to be able to play because at any minute you can lose your career, and while I play, as many days as God gives me, I'm going to make sure I go 100 percent.'"

With Lin leading the way the following season, the team began winning . . . and winning big. He was running the show from the point by showing a great basketball IQ and keeping his teammates involved in the offense, while scoring enough to be considered a threat. His coach, Peter Diepenbrock, had been touting Lin's ability since his junior year. His individual skills aside, Diepenbrock said he had the same two priorities every time he took the court:

"He just thought about making plays and winning games," Diepenbrock said. "It was uncanny. You could bank on him every time."

Diepenbrock went on to say that he felt Jeremy was a special player even before he came to Palo Alto as a 5'3" freshman. "He was a youth league legend out here," the coach said. He even brought his little guard up to the varsity level during the playoffs of his freshman year. "He nailed a key, three-pointer down the stretch in his first game. After that, he never stopped making them."

Diepenbrock likes to rattle off the numerous highlights of Jeremy's senior year when the Palo Alto Vikings would go 32-1 and win the state title. He starts with the semifinal game of the Santa Cruz Dad's Tournament against St. Francis: "We're down a bucket in the final minute of overtime and Jeremy hits a twenty-five-footer. We win, 57-55." Next was the consolation game of the Mission Prep Classic against Backerfield: "We're down three with five seconds left. [Jeremy] catches the inbounds pass, penetrates [the lane], kicks it out, and Steven Brown drills a three-pointer at the buzzer. We win 80-74 in overtime and Jeremy has a triple-double."

In the NorCal semifinals against Luguna Creek, Lin struck again: "We're up two, their stud, Brandon Adams, gets the ball underneath in the final seconds. Jeremy rips the ball out of his hands, gets fouled, and hits the free throw. We win, 54-51." Then in the NorCal finals against Mitty at the Arco Arena, Palo Alto was down one with 24.1 seconds to play: "Lin draws two defenders and finds Brad Lehman, who drills a three-pointer from the corner. We win, 45-43, and [Lin] makes it look easy."

Finally, it was time for the California Interscholastic Federation Division II title game against Mater Dei, a private school that was nationally ranked and heavily favored. Once again, Jeremy Lin ran the show, handing the ball, passing deftly, and showing his usual fearlessness when he went to the hoop, drawing defenders to him and freeing up teammates for a kick-out pass. As happens so often, the game came down to the final seconds . . . and once more, Peter Diepenbrock remembers:

"We're up two with thirty seconds left. [Lin] decides to drive the basket. He takes on their star, Taylor King, goes over him, and makes a layup to ice it."

The state title seemed like icing on cake, completing a great year for the slim guard with the unbreakable will to win. For the season, Jeremy averaged 15.1 points a game, adding 7.1 assists, 6.2 rebounds, and 5.0 steals. The numbers might not have been as eye-popping as other big prospects, but they certainly showed a well-rounded and complete game. That was validated when Jeremy was named not only first-team All State, but Northern California Division II Player of the Year as well.

Californian Chuck Leung, who also happens to be Asian American and plays basketball, caught a replay of that championship game in 2006 on television and was immediately struck by the play of Jeremy Lin. He described it thus:

> I was quickly riveted by a skinny, Taiwanese kid from Palo Alto, who repeatedly herked and jerked his way into the paint for points, leading his undersized team to a dramatic victory over heavily favored Mater Dei. Even then, Jeremy Lin's game couldn't exactly be described as pretty. But he refused to shy away from either pressure or contact in the biggest games—against the biggest dudes—he had probably played in his life.

Jeremy's high school days were over. As expected, he had done exceedingly well with his studies, compiling the kind of grades that would give him a wide choice of top colleges. Yet he was also in love with basketball and also wanted to continue at the next level. And therein was the problem.

Recruitment, or the Lack Thereof

The recruiting process for any top high school athlete, especially in basketball and football, can be an exciting, thrilling, and sometimes nerve-racking experience. With all the major colleges on the prowl for the best players, recruiters are armed with full-boat scholarship offers and sometimes even a little extra. The smart players stay away from the extras, but not the opportunity to play for a top program and hopefully take their skills to the next level—the NBA or NFL. All too few student-athletes in today's world complete their four years, as well as graduate with college degrees. The top collegiate players know that there is an opportunity for fame and fortune if things go right, and it all starts with the recruiting process.

Unfortunately, for Jeremy Lin, there was virtually no recruiting process at all, and for a variety of reasons. There was no question about where he wanted to go. Being a California kid, he wanted to stay at home and play in the PAC-10, preferably at UCLA, where his older brother Josh was a student. But since nothing was certain and no recruiters had approached him, he sent a résumé and a highlight DVD of his high school career to UCLA, the University of California at Berkeley, and Stanford University, located right in his backyard and one of the finest academic institutions in the country. Because of his outstanding grades and desire to complete his education, he also sent his résumé to all the Ivy League Schools.

But why hadn't any of these schools approached *him*? Rex Walters was a former NBA player who was then coaching at the University of San Francisco. Walters felt that NCAA limits on coaches' recruiting visits had hurt Jeremy's chances:

"Most colleges start recruiting a guy in the first five minutes they see him, usually because of how fast he runs, how high he jumps, and the quickness he shows them. These are the easy things to evaluate." In other words, none of those "easy things" were apparent with Jeremy Lin.

Harvard assistant coach Bill Holden had first seen Jeremy in July of 2005. He, too, was not initially impressed with Lin's on-court abilities, and he told Pete Diepenbrock that he thought Jeremy could only succeed as a Division III player.

"I was the West Coast recruiter for Harvard at the time," Holden said, "and the first time I saw him it just wasn't a good game to evaluate. The opponent he played against that night wasn't very strong. It wasn't a good overall game and that's what led me to say he was only ready for Division III. A couple of days later I saw him in another gym in a high level AAU game against a very competitive team that included several Division I athletes. There were a number of college coaches watching and Jeremy was just a totally different player. He was rising to the occasion—the high level of the other team—and was showing all his natural basketball instincts, especially the ability to read things. He also played great defense and was getting to the hoop and scoring consistently. In a nutshell, he was showing me things that often can't be taught. He had the instincts of a killer and immediately became my top priority as our number one recruit for Harvard."

Peter Diepenbrock initially felt that the fact that Jeremy was an Asian American wouldn't affect his recruiting, but that perception changed when he saw some ten Division I coaches scouting an African American Palo Alto player he felt "could have been a nice junior college player."

"That's when I'm thinking, there might be something to this," Diepenbrock said. "If [Lin] was African American or Caucasian, it might have been a different deal." If true, the reason would seem to be that college coaches and recruiters just didn't feel an Asian American was ready for big time college ball. After all, there were virtually none of them playing and there were zero in the NBA.

Though he had been growing steadily, Jeremy was still just 6'1" and maybe 170 pounds when he finished his high school career. There was no way of knowing he would grow another two inches and add some thirty-five additional pounds of strength and muscle to his body. Before his growth spurt, his size worked against him. Even Pete Diepenbrock admitted, "I wasn't sitting there saying all these Division I coaches were knuckleheads. There were legitimate questions about Jeremy."

The larger Division I schools in the area barely gave him lip service. He would later say that Stanford was only "fake interested" in him. And he probably saw the handwriting on the wall when one of the staffers at the University of California called him by the wrong name, referring to him as Ron.

"Everybody was pretty much on the same page, the wrong page," Diepenbrock said. "I was even thinking the same thing. Basically, it was an issue of size and strength. You just can't predict how intangible skills are going to translate to the next level. It's easy to predict the 6'5" guy who can jump through the roof. If he can jump through the roof in high school, he can also do it in college. But for a person that doesn't have those types of physical skills, it's harder to predict how it's going to translate."

Only two California schools, St. Mary's and Santa Clara, might have come the closest to offering scholarships, but didn't. UCLA passed, as did Stanford. The best UCLA would offer was the opportunity to make the team as a walk-on. Later, Kerry Keating, the UCLA assistant who made the walk-on offer, said that Jeremy probably would have ended up the team's starting point guard. And Joe Lacob, who would become the owner of the Golden State Warriors and who was a Stanford booster, said Stanford's failure to recruit Lin, who was playing virtually across the street, was "really stupid," adding, "The kid was right across the street. If you can't recognize that, you've got a problem." But they didn't.

As for Jeremy, he felt that he had the answer to what might have held him back. "I just think, in order for someone to understand my game, they have to watch me more than once," he said, "because I'm not going to do anything that's extra flashy or freakishly athletic." Those words would prove to be prophetic when he would look to start an NBA career some four years later.

After all the applications and rejections from the West Coast schools, his final decision came down to Harvard or Brown, a pair of Ivy League schools. They were the only two that pretty much guaranteed him a spot on their teams. But with no athletic scholarships, he'd have to pursue aide as a student, and with his 4.2 GPA, that was most certainly workable. He finally chose Harvard and would be coming east to Massachusetts in the fall of 2006. He would study economics and play basketball, pursuing both with his usual tenacity and desire to excel.

Bill Holden, the Harvard recruiter who eventually made Jeremy his number one priority, would later detail more of the reasons he convinced the Ivy League school to grab Lin.

The thing that really drew me to Jeremy was that he just had some natural basketball instincts that you can't coach. He just had a good way of reading the game, a good vision of the game, and a good understanding of the game. He had that as a senior in high school and those are things that aren't coachable. He already had a knack for doing them.

Recruiters for the highest level programs are looking for guys that are already physically developed. Some today even want guys who they know will be one year and done, and then onto the NBA. They want guys who will make an immediate impact in their program. Maybe they just couldn't foresee that in Jeremy. He already had foot speed coming out of high school, but certainly couldn't dunk the ball as he would later do at Harvard. No one knew how much more he would grow and that he'd develop a work ethic in the weight room to strengthen his body and make himself better. So he was difficult to project.

Holden also said that he saw a very respectful young man and someone with a sincere interest in attending Harvard. He also saw the inner ego that most top athletes have, one that made him think he could play at an even higher level than Harvard. In other words, he had a very strong belief in himself.

Despite wanting Lin for Harvard, Bill Holden said he wasn't surprised that Jeremy didn't receive any scholarship offers, especially from the big schools. "He was still not physically a Division I recruit at that time," he recalled. "While he had a tremendous senior year, he didn't have the kind of work ethic that he would eventually develop. Harvard was the right place for him in that he would have four years to fully develop. Had he gone to a big time school he may not have gotten off the bench much and never developed as a player. And he most likely wouldn't have started.

"I projected him as a possible all-league player by his junior or senior year. He already had the capability to make some plays that most other kids can't make at the Ivy League level. He wasn't consistent with it yet, but he had the potential to grow into those things, develop his jump shot and work on his body. What he had was the intangibles that make us feel we just have to have this kid."

So it was off to Harvard. Maybe he wasn't going to UCLA, USC, or Stanford, but he was going to one of the best colleges in the country where the opportunity to get a top education was as good as anywhere else. Harvard grads are always looked upon as special. And, oh yes, there was basketball. When it came to the court, Jeremy Lin was still anxious to prove himself. He would have to go the extra mile once again. It wasn't the first time, and certainly wouldn't be the last.

Chapter Two: From Harvard to . . . Where?

THE MAJORITY OF students going to Ivy League schools are there for one reason and one reason only: to get the aforementioned top education. Graduate from Harvard, Yale, Princeton, or any other Ivy League school, and you should already have a leg up on life. Athletics at this level are almost incidental. Because there are no athletic scholarships, the top high school players will mostly shun the Ivy Leagues with a few choice exceptions, such as former Knick, Rhodes Scholar, and U.S. senator, Bill Bradley. But by and large, those going to a school such as Harvard harbor no thoughts of a professional sports career.

Though Jeremy Lin certainly had a real love of basketball and fully intended to play for the Crimson, he was also a realist. While the NBA might have been in the back of his mind when he first went to Harvard, it certainly wasn't "Plan A." That plan was to stay for four years and earn a degree, then let the basketball chips fall where they may.

Unlike some of the large universities that warehouse athletes and build their programs to earn millions of dollars, Harvard continues to put an emphasis on education. An education is available for those who want it at every institution, but the harsh reality is that many top athletes use college as a training ground for what they hope is the next step—the pros— and some of these universities use the athletes to keep their programs nationally ranked, hoping for a bid to a bowl game or the NCAA Tournament. At stake—besides school pride— are millions of dollars. Harvard, of course, wasn't like that. At Cambridge, Jeremy lived a dual existence: He was a student participating in all aspects of Harvard life, and an athlete, trying to become the best basketball player he could be.

All incoming Harvard freshmen must live in or adjacent to Harvard Yard on the campus, but, beginning the following year, students can choose to live with friends as part of the housing system. With his life steeped in academics, religion, and basketball, Jeremy had a tight-knit group of friends—some athletes, others students—and they spent three years together at Leverett House, overlooking the Charles River, which separates Cambridge from Boston. Cheng Ho was a close friend of Jeremy and participated in his weekly Bible study group at the school.

"[Jeremy] was the leader of the group—" Cheng recalls, "organized and prepared everything. We would go through the verses he would print out for each of us, review them, and then talk about the meaning and how it all applies to our lives. But at the same time we had a lot of fun. Jeremy was just a regular guy—often a goofball. He always had a great sense of humor and would often say things that surprised me."

Doug Miller, who was the team's co-captain with Jeremy when they were seniors, was part of the Leverett House group.

He remembers it as a nice mix of athletes, artists, and others. Several of the players took economics classes together and helped each other with their studies. He and Jeremy often studied together on road trips. As mentioned, academics were always number one at Harvard.

Another of his former teammates, Alek Blankenau, remembers the one time he saw Jeremy get flustered, on or off the court. It was when they were freshmen waiting to get flu shots. Though Blankenau didn't know it at the time, Jeremy always had a fear of needles.

"Everyone was in line, real nonchalant," Blankenau remembered, "and I looked back and noticed that Jeremy seemed extremely distressed, not anything like the cool, calm, and collected guy I had grown to know. That's when he said to me, 'I think we should just get out of line and leave.' I asked him if he was serious. I told him he had to get it together. It was definitely the most flustered I'd ever seen him."

Blankenau also remembered a Valentine's Day when Jeremy forgot to make a dinner reservation for himself and a girl he was dating at the time. "He wasn't much of a guy to cook things, so his roommates helped out and put together a pretty nice meal for them."

Cheng Ho said their lives at Harvard were pretty typical of many college guys. "We would go to parties, talk to girls, and meet people," Cheng related. "We just didn't take things to the next level. I was a better dancer than he was, so I would try to teach him to dance."

Alek Blankenau remembers Jeremy as always being "very focused on basketball." But religion also played a major role in his life. Jeremy always stayed true to his feelings, but never pushed his beliefs on others.

"I went to church with him a few times," Blankenau said. "He'd always encourage you to come along, but if I said no, it was fine with him. I never saw him pressure anyone when it came to religion."

Cheng Ho was born in Taiwan before coming to Georgia at the age of thirteen. He was a running back on the Harvard football team, so he and Jeremy came together as athletes with an Asian heritage. Cheng was only marginally interested in religion before Jeremy invited him to join a study group, which consisted of six to eight people, with the sessions usually lasting an hour or two.

"The way he thinks and believes is very consistent," Cheng said, "and it's very contagious to be around him. I think what he has is a gift."

Doug Miller said Jeremy was always happy to talk about religion, but only if another person wanted to talk about it. "But he was just as willing to talk about Halo (a popular video game) if that's what the other person wanted. We would also talk about girls or girl problems, video games, classes, or politics. He's a pretty smart guy."

Christopher Foote was a Harvard professor who had Jeremy in his intermediate macro course his sophomore year. He's never forgotten his attentiveness and his excellent attendance at his three-times-a-week lectures. It was a 9:00 AM class and Foote said that many students would skip it from time to time.

"I remember exactly where [Jeremy] sat, up in the balcony to my right," Professor Foote said. "My impression is that he was not just thinking about basketball all the time. He was trying to make the most of the advantages Harvard could give him."

There was little doubt about that. Jeremy always kept his grades up and graduated with an outstanding grade point average. There was never any thought of leaving school early. Even if he had been considered a top basketball prospect, which he wasn't, he would have stayed to finish what he had started.

On the Basketball Court

Jeremy was a part timer his freshman year, coming off the bench and learning the system. He averaged just 4.8 points a game and knew he had to work on his shot. His field goal percentage was at 41.5, which wasn't good enough. Harvard finished his freshman season with a 13-14 record. But Jeremy had shown enough skill and enough improvement to earn the starting point guard spot as a sophomore in 2007–2008. Lemar Reddicks, who helped recruit Jeremy and who left Harvard to become an assistant at Boston College, always felt the youngster from Palo Alto would be a good player, but recalled him as a "weak string bean" when he first came to Harvard. Jeremy, however, worked hard, and by his senior year was said to be the team's strongest player.

Despite Jeremy's modest stats as a freshman, Bill Holden was one who felt that he would make his mark before his Harvard career ended.

"Even as a freshman he had an ability to get to the basket, to get into the lane and score," Holden said. "That's something he would always be able to do. He was unique in the sense that you usually have offensive players that are drivers and offensive players that are shooters. Well, he was kind of a unique player in that he had the mid-range game where he could get to the foul line and pull up and elevate over smaller defenders and score. That was probably the best thing he did his first year. I was singing his praises as a freshman, saying that in the future he would be very good."

Tommy Amaker became Harvard's new head coach in 2007–2008. Amaker had been a point guard at Duke, and then as an assistant with the Blue Devils before getting head coaching experience at Seton Hall and Michigan. It was a season in which the team struggled, but began putting things together for the future. Though Harvard was just 8-22, Jeremy's game began coming of age. He averaged 12.6 points in thirty games, adding 4.8 rebounds, 3.6 assists, and 1.9 steals a game. For his efforts, he was named All-Ivy League Second Team. According Bill Holden, he wasn't strictly a point guard then.

"His role slowly changed during his Harvard career," Holden said, "but he didn't necessarily play point guard the way he does now. There was sometimes another point guard on the court with him, but he certainly had the ball in his hands quite a bit. As a freshman, he was the first guard off the bench, became a starter as a sophomore, and then developed into an all-league player. I would define him as a slashing-type scoring guard with great ability to get to the rim and a great ability to get fouled. He has a strong sense of the game, the vision to see his teammates, and his defensive game improved steadily during the years he played at Harvard."

There was one game during his sophomore year that perhaps pointed to the kind of high character person he was. The Crimson traveled to Boston to play Boston University where his former coach and recruiter, Lemar Reddicks, was then an assistant. As the players warmed up before the game, Jeremy went to the sideline and began to talk with Reddicks.

"He comes up to me and he doesn't leave," Reddicks recalled. "Finally, I'm like, 'Jeremy, go get warmed up, man, you've got a game.' And he goes, 'Coach, I have thirty games this year. I only have one where I get to see you, so I'm going to spend as much time as I can with you.' Believe it or not, my eyes started to water."

Jeremy and the team began to come of age in the 2008–2009 season. While Harvard did not ordinarily play nationally-ranked schools, the opening game of the previous season was against Stanford, then ranked 23rd in the country. Harvard was blown out 111-56. So when they met 17th ranked Boston College on January 7, most expected another big loss. BC was coming off an upset victory over North Carolina, the nation's top team, and the Eagles were flying high . . . until they met a junior guard named Jeremy Lin.

All Jeremy did that night was score 27 points, adding eight assists and six steals. Defensively, he held BC's all-American guard, Tyrese Rice, scoreless in the first half as his team built a 33-27 lead. Rice was coming off a 25-point game against North Carolina. Jeremy eventually fouled out with 40 seconds left and actually received a respectful round of applause by the BC fans. When it ended, Harvard had an 82-70 victory, which was their first-ever win against the nationally ranked opponent.

"That game was something I'll never forget, an emotional high," Jeremy said. "It was something our players and coaches deserved. We've all worked very hard. We earned it."

"Obviously, it's a special night for us and for our basketball program," Coach Amaker said, afterward. "To be able to come across town and play against and outstanding basketball team, especially after what they experienced in their previous game."

It seemed whenever BC began making a run, Jeremy would isolate against whichever defender was trying to stop him and drive to the lane; either scoring himself, getting fouled, or setting up a teammate.

"He got in a rhythm," was the way BC coach Al Skinner described it.

Jeremy exhibited great poise throughout the game, from calmly hitting a three-pointer from the left corner to give the Crimson its first double-digit lead, 42-31, with 16:55 left to play in the second half, to making sure his team stayed in control in the closing minutes. He had simply played a great, all-around game and helped to put Harvard on the basketball map.

By the middle of the month, Harvard had a modest, 9-6, record, but Jeremy was starting to make his mark. He was the only collegian in the country who ranked among the top ten players in his conference in points, rebounds, assists, steals, blocks, field-goal percentage, free-throw percentage, and three-point shooting percentage, which is an incredible achievement in itself. At that point in the season, he was averaging 17.9 points and 5.5 rebounds a game . . . not bad for a 6'3" guard. Always self-effacing and ready to give credit rather than take it, Jeremy was quick to cite his teammates for part of his success.

"When all the other guys on the floor are doing a good job defending, that can force a bad pass and I can grab the ball," he said. "I'm trying to do whatever the team needs me to do in a particular game. A lot of the time, it's not going to be scoring, even though that's what is most valued when people talk about a game. Sometimes it's going to be rebounding or passing. It's a credit to the other guys on our team that I don't have to be scoring every game. We have several players who can score."

Coach Amaker was quickly becoming a Lin admirer. Looking back over his nineteen years of coaching experience, he said, "I haven't coached anyone I would regard higher [than Lin]. Jeremy is a hard worker, a passionate ballplayer, a student of the game who really loves to play. He's an unselfish young man, sometimes to a fault. Jeremy's a complete player, a throwback to the days of yesteryear. He could play basketball in any era, and I love coaching him. It's great to have a player you sometimes have to ask to slow down, instead of 'Please, take it up a notch.'"

By his senior year, there was no longer any doubt about Jeremy's ability. He continued to work hard at all phases of the game and somewhere deep down inside he had to be thinking about the next level—the NBA. But that dream was something that he wouldn't talk about openly. He just wanted his team to win and continued to work hard at his studies while enjoying the final year of college life. It had obviously been a wonderful experience for him.

As his final season got underway, Jeremy talked about what the Harvard basketball experience had meant to him. For openers, he was named a co-captain of the team, something he took very seriously.

"Obviously, it's an honor and a privilege to be able to be a captain," he said. "It's not something that we take lightly and it's a once-in-a-lifetime opportunity. We try to lead by example and come out here and set the pace and push everybody."

Over the summer he had played in the San Francisco Pro-Am, an NCAA sanctioned summer league, explaining that he had played strictly point guard and "focused on my passing and ball-handling and becoming a better playmaker. Here, I have more of a scoring role so it should help me with my play making. That experience will help if teams are doubling and using ball-screens, things like that."

He also had praise for his coach, Tommy Amaker. "It's really humbling sometimes, when you look at his résumé, he's accomplished a lot, and I'm still kind of shocked that I get to be coached by someone like that every day. Everybody respects him when he speaks. There's no doubt that he's our leader and the head of our program."

As for his choice of Harvard and the overall basketball experience, he couldn't have been happier. "It's been an awesome experience," he said. "I couldn't have asked for anything better. It has been a pleasure to be here. I didn't imagine my career going the way it has. I'm really blessed to be in this situation. We are creating a family atmosphere and the guys all enjoy being around each other. We're all really close off the basketball court, as well. In terms of the game we know we have not accomplished what we wanted in the past, and we (the seniors) have one year to accomplish those goals. We'd like to start hanging some banners here."

The Crimson had finished his junior year at 14-14, but was now a winning team en route to a 21-8 record with Jeremy Lin at the helm. He was finally getting some notice. Former college coach and ESPN analyst Fran Fraschilla included him on a list of the twelve most versatile players in college basketball. As he had done against Boston College the year before, Jeremy played perhaps his best game as a senior against the 12th ranked University of Connecticut. Though Harvard lost, he equaled his career high with 30 points and grabbed nine big rebounds against the taller, more physical Huskies team. After the game, UConn coach Jim Calhoun made it a point to talk about Jeremy.

"I've seen a lot of teams come through here, and he could play for any of them," the Hall of Fame coach said. "He's got great, great composure on the court. He simply knows how to play."

At season's end, Harvard had taken a huge step toward establishing its basketball program. Not that it was ever going to be a Kentucky or Kansas, North Carolina or Duke, but the student-athlete with basketball skills would now take a harder look thanks, in part, to the success that Jeremy Lin had and the record of Tommy Amaker's 2009–2010 team.

Jeremy averaged 16.4 points a game his senior year, adding 4.4 rebounds and 4.5 assists. Some of his numbers were down slightly from the year before, but the team was better, showing once again that he always thought team-first and played for the win, not for his stats. However, he was one of thirty midseason candidates for the prestigious John R. Wooden Award and one of eleven finalists for the Bob Cousy Award, given to the best point guard in the land. He was a unanimous choice for the All-Ivy League first team and finished his career as the first player in Ivy League history to record at least 1,450 points, 450 rebounds, 400 assists, and 200 steals.

His success wasn't handed to him. It was the result of good old-fashioned hard work. Former teammate Oliver McNally confirmed that when he said, "He was the hardest working guy we had even when he was the best player we had here. On top of that, he's an extremely humble, down-to-earth guy, and this kind of success couldn't have happened to a better person."

Needless to say, he also graduated with his degree in economics. And that begged the question, what next?

. . .

WITH A DEGREE from Harvard, Jeremy was certainly in a position to move on without basketball. Jeff Foote, who played for Cornell, also had his eyes on the NBA. He ended up playing with teams in Israel, Spain, and Poland, made an appearance in the Portland Trail Blazers' camp, and then went to the Springfield Armor in the D-League. Obviously, Foote loves the game but knows he always has his college degree to fall back upon.

"The good thing about going to an Ivy League school is that you've got a lot of options after getting your degree," Foote said, "and a lot of them are more lucrative than basketball, especially for someone who is where I'm at. You get a good starting salary with, say, Goldman Sachs or Morgan Stanley, and maybe ten or twenty years down the road you wind up even better off. The bad thing is that people assumed you played in the Ivy League because you weren't good enough to get an athletic scholarship anywhere else."

There was a lot of truth in what Foote said and definitely some preconceived notions about Ivy League players. They

weren't looked upon the same way as guys coming out of
Kentucky, Michigan State, Duke, or UConn—schools that
regularly produced players who found success in the NBA. Ivy
Leaguers playing at the top level were few and far between. In
fact, when Jeremy came out in 2010, the last Ivy League player
selected in the NBA draft was Jerome Allen of Penn in 1995.
The last Ivy Leaguer to actually play in the NBA was Yale's
Chris Dudley, who retired in 2003. Even more amazing, the
last Harvard basketball player to actually wear an NBA uniform was Ed Smith, way back in 1954. So Jeremy Lin knew
right away that the odds were against him; but being a positive
person, he set his sights on the next level. He wanted a chance
to test himself against the best in the NBA.

Chapter Three: A Time of Frustration

ON **NOVEMBER 15,** 2009, Harvard was playing William & Mary. It was a close game that would eventually go into triple-overtime, the kind of nail-biter that keeps fans on the edge of their seats. It ended in the last second of the third overtime when Jeremy hit a shot just before the buzzer to give Harvard an 87-85 victory. It was a big win coming early in the season and one of those who left impressed with Jeremy's performance was the William & Mary coach, Tony Shaver.

Two days earlier, Shaver's team had opened the season against the University of Connecticut, one of the best teams in the land. The Connecticut backcourt of Kemba Walker and Jerome Dyson torched William & Mary for a combined 39 points, 10 assists, and six steals as UConn won 75-66. Yet, after playing Harvard and losing in triple overtime, Tony Shaver had a thought that would have surprised a lot of people.

"[Walker and Dyson] were terrific," he said, "but I honestly thought Jeremy Lin was better. He was 6'3" and extremely athletic, which most people didn't believe. He played the ball screen as well as anybody I've ever seen, using the ball screen to score. I thought he was a guy who definitely should get an NBA look, I really did."

Not only did Shaver think that Jeremy should get a look, but he did something about it. He called his college suitemate at North Carolina, Mitch Kupchak, a former NBA player who was the general manager of the Los Angeles Lakers, and he pretty much raved about Lin.

"My only hesitation, and I also told it to Mitch, was that I wasn't sure he was a good enough shooter. A lot of times a 6'3" guard has to be a phenomenal shooter. But I really thought he deserved a look."

Despite the personal recommendation from an old friend, Kupchak and the Lakers would pass on Lin when the draft rolled around. It was a theme that would soon become all too familiar. Eight teams did invite Jeremy to pre-draft workouts, but the workouts often did not include full court five-on-five play. Jeremy himself said the workouts were mostly "one-on-one, two-on-two, three-on-three, and that's not where I excel. I've never played basketball like that." As Bill Holden had said four years earlier, Jeremy played his best against the best in the biggest games and toughest situations.

It wasn't looking good. He certainly wasn't considered a blue-chip prospect, and thus, pretty much seemed off the radar. Part of it might have been that he played in the Ivy League, not considered by most as a high-level conference. Another part might have been his heritage. Very few players of Asian heritage or Asian American heritage have played in the NBA, and unfortunately there had to have been some sense of a preconceived notion that he didn't have the necessary athleticism to make the final transition. The NBA draft came and went, and Jeremy wasn't chosen. But he still wasn't ready to give up, and neither were several NBA teams.

The Dallas Mavericks eventually invited him to a mini-camp and then asked him to play in a summer league. He played both point and shooting guard in five summer league games, averaging 9.8 points, 1.8 assists, and 3.2 rebounds, all while leading the team with a 54.5 shooting percentage . . . and did that while averaging just 18.6 minutes on the floor. Obviously, something was there, but the question was, did anyone see it? He did impress observers when he played against the league's top draft pick, John Wall. Wall scored 21 points to Lin's 13, but Jeremy hit 6 of 12 shots in twenty-eight minutes, while Wall connected on just 4 of 19 in thirty-three minutes.

Finally, four teams apparently had seen enough to step forward with offers: the Dallas Mavericks, Los Angeles Lakers, and an unnamed Eastern Conference team were ready to ante up first; and then the Golden State Warriors followed with an offer. On July 21, 2010, Jeremy signed a two-year deal with the hometown Warriors, his favorite team while growing up in Palo Alto. The deal was only partially guaranteed for the 2010–2011 season with the team holding an option for the second year. His first year salary was close to $500,000, with more than half of it being guaranteed. Jeremy later said the three other teams had made slightly higher offers, but he wanted to play for the Warriors because the team was so close to home. He also signed a three-year guaranteed contract with Nike, and his jersey was put on sale before he had played his first NBA game.

So it wasn't quite as bleak a situation as some now believe. The opportunity was there, though it isn't easy for a guy not considered a top prospect to grab it. He often just doesn't get a real chance unless he's so good that he simply cannot be denied. But by being signed, even to the league minimum, he would be earning more than most college graduates on their first job. And that held true whether the college was Harvard or some community college in the Midwest. Professional athletes today are exceedingly well paid, even the unproven rookies.

However, this good fortune would not necessarily continue unless he was able to establish himself. Because the San Francisco Bay Area already had a large Asian American population, Jeremy had something of a "cult following" even before his first game. He was also the first American of Chinese or Taiwanese descent to ever play in the NBA, and those fans knew it. Not surprisingly, he received the loudest cheers from a crowd of 10,004 fans who attended the Warriors first preseason game at the Oracle Arena. They cheered for him in warm-ups and cheered even louder when he entered the game in the fourth quarter.

"That was something that really touched me," Jeremy would say. "It's something I'll remember forever."

He didn't play badly, scoring seven points, grabbing three rebounds, and handing out two assists in eleven minutes of action. The support from the Asian community continued and so did the expectations. People wanted to see him excel, even star; but he was more realistic, telling people, "I won't be an All-Star this year," adding, "I still haven't proven anything to anyone." One writer even mentioned that he seemed to have occasional "seeds of self-doubt," something quite uncommon for most NBA players. When once asked which player he could compare himself to, Jeremy surprised a lot of people by pointing to Goran Dragic, a backup point guard with the Phoenix Suns.

"Neither of us is a freak athlete," he said, "but we're both effective and know how to play the game."

Because of his heritage, he was receiving many requests for interviews, but the team tried to limit them so he could concentrate on his game and keep his focus. He made the club's opening day roster, an accomplishment in itself, but was firmly rooted to the end of the bench. In fact, he was placed on the inactive list for the opening game, commenting that "part of being on this team is putting your ego aside." It had to be a difficult time for someone used to having the ball in his hands for a good part of the game, as he had for three years at Harvard.

When he was activated, he found himself playing behind the team's two top guards, Stephen Curry and Monta Ellis, while competing with Charlie Bell, Reggie Williams and, later in the season, Acie Law IV for playing time. His NBA debut came in the second game of the season, which also happened to be Asian Heritage Night, and he received a standing ovation from the crowd of 17,408 fans when he came out on the floor with just 2:32 remaining in the fourth quarter. He didn't score, but got himself into the NBA stat book with one steal. It was the official beginning of his career, but there was still a very big question about how long it would last.

Jeremy managed his first basket in the team's next game against the Lakers and had three assists, and his ballhawking on defense resulted in four steals. He even got a big hand from the crowd at the Staples Center in Los Angeles. On the down side, he also committed five fouls in only sixteen minutes, but Coach Keith Smart praised him, saying "Lin came in and did a good job, gave us a good tempo." Lakers' guard Derek Fisher also praised the rookie for his energy and aggressiveness.

Surprisingly, Jeremy seemed a bit unnerved when the Warriors played at home. There was always a large contingent of Asian American fans at the Oracle Arena and they cheered every time he touched the basketball. Teammate Stephen Curry was one who saw it repeatedly.

"There's a lot of pressure on him at home with all the applause for just checking into the game," Curry said. "So I'm sure that cranks up the nerves just a little bit. You can tell he plays a lot better on the road because he can just go out there, play, and have fun."

Coach Smart also noticed that Jeremy looked more relaxed on the road, and he himself admitted, "When I'm on the road, I don't feel like the spotlight is on me."

But even on the road there could be pressure. The Warriors were slated to play in Toronto on November 8, and the Raptors decided to hold an Asian Heritage Night to coincide with his appearance. There were some twenty members of Toronto's Chinese media covering the game. At Madison Square Garden against the Knicks, ESPN.com NBA editor Matt Wong noted that "Lin checked into the game to loud applause, presumably from the many Asian Americans in attendance." It was apparent that Jeremy had become a source of pride for Asian Americans, who never had one of their own in the NBA before. Because he was only playing a few minutes a game, there was added pressure for him to make his mark whenever he stepped onto the court. He did manage 13 points in eighteen minutes against the Lakers in Los Angeles and once again was cheered loudly by the crowd.

But as the season wore on, it became more apparent that he was a fringe player who wasn't moving up from that end spot on the bench. On three occasions during the season, the team sent him down to their D-League affiliate, the Reno Bighorns, only to recall him a short time later. But with Reno, he excelled, averaging 18.0 points, 5.8 rebounds, and 4.3 assists a game. He had a high of 27 points in a March 18 game with the Bighorns, but it wasn't the NBA. It still felt like a demotion. Even so, he also realized that he was getting playing time in the D-League that he wouldn't have received with the Warriors, and he eventually praised the Bighorns coach, Eric Musselman, for "helping me regain my swagger."

Warriors owner Joe Lacob would admit he received more than one trade offer for Jeremy during the season, but the team turned them all down. They were happy with Jeremy's progress as an undrafted free agent. "He's a minimum, inexpensive asset," was the way Lacob put it. "You need to look at him as a developing asset. Is he going to be a superstar? No."

That was the bottom line. Jeremy had the start of an NBA career . . . but barely. In twenty-nine games with the Warriors, he averaged 2.6 points on just 38.9 percent shooting, which, sadly, wasn't good enough. With the agreement between the Players Association and the owners set to expire, there was the threat of a lockout that could hold up or even postpone the start of the next season, so Jeremy was in a kind of limbo. The team hadn't picked up his option for the 2011–2012 campaign and there was certainly no guarantee that they would. So once again a familiar question loomed: "What next?"

Sure enough, a contentious lockout threatened the upcoming season as both sides argued about how to divide the money. The owners claimed too many teams were losing money and demanded the players lower the percentage of revenue they were getting. The players, on the other hand, felt the owners were squeezing them, so hard feelings prevailed on both sides as each tried to woo the media and fans into thinking they were the good guys. In the meantime, players were left without many options. There could be no trades, no signings, no team workouts, and use of team facilities was forbidden. For a fringe player like Jeremy Lin, the lockout could have been a kiss of death.

Jeremy had to take it slow over the summer, giving him time to allow a knee injury to heal. That September, with the lockout continuing, he traveled to China and played several games with the Dongguan Leopards of the Chinese Basketball Association in Guangzhou. This was during the championship tournament, and he was promptly named the Tourney MVP. That's when the Shanghai Sharks, whose president was former NBA star Yao Ming, tried to sign him for the next season. Jeremy was technically still under contract with Golden State and pointed out that the CBA could only sign NBA free agents. In November, he considered signing with a team in Italy, but that was rendered moot when the NBA lockout ended on November 26.

Though Jeremy had worked hard to improve his jump shot during the off-season, he never had a chance to show it to the Warriors. The team had a new coach in former star point guard, Mark Jackson, but Jeremy didn't get the opportunity to display his wares. The team waived him on December 9, the first day of training camp, so they could free up some salary cap money to make an offer to free agent center DeAndre Jordan, who would later sign with the Los Angeles Clippers. There was also an article in the *San Francisco Chronicle* that basically said Jeremy was cut because he would have had trouble beating out rookie guard Charles Jenkins.

Had Jeremy stayed with the team until February 10, his salary of $800,000 would have become fully guaranteed. Now he had nothing—no salary and no team. Luckily for him, he wasn't a free agent for long. On December 12, he was claimed off waivers by the Houston Rockets. There was hope yet again.

Houston's General Manager, Daryl Morey, had met Jeremy on a hotel elevator at the 2010 Portsmouth Invitational Tournament and was intrigued by the former Harvard star. Morey, an MIT graduate, said the team had a deep scouting profile on Lin as well as a personal interest. The Rockets were the team that 7'6" center Yao Ming had played for before his premature retirement due to recurring foot injuries. Yao, of course, was a Chinese national, and Morey saw the connection, especially when Jeremy asked him questions about Yao that sparked a discussion between the two.

The Portsmouth Invitational took place in the spring of Jeremy's senior year at Harvard and was a venue where so-called fringe prospects come to impress NBA scouts prior to the draft. Morey remembered a great deal of doubt in the young man.

"He was so unsure. He wondered if he would even get an invite to a training camp," Morey said.

He had a good reason. Fringe prospects are looking for one thing: a chance. They never know if they will get it and, if they do, whether they will be given a real chance to show their talents. In this case, the Rockets already had three point guards with guaranteed contracts: Kyle Lowry, Goran Dragic, and Jonny Flynn. Jeremy ended up playing just seven minutes in two preseason games with the Rockets and, on December 24, just before the start of the season, was waived for a familiar reason—to clear payroll so the team could sign center Samuel Dalembert. His stay with the Rockets lasted all of twelve days. Later, GM Morey said a curious thing:

"Even if he had stayed here we probably wouldn't have recognized his talent as much as we should have. He probably wouldn't have played much at all, and then would have been released at the end of the year. I didn't know he could play this well and, if I did, we would have kept him."

How could so many teams not see the innate talent and at least allow the player a chance to translate it to the court via playing time? After all, there are always players who combine positive intangibles with that talent, and that's the thing that can make it all work. But it won't if they aren't given enough of a chance.

"I talk to other GMs about this all the time," Morey said. "This is how our coach, Kevin McHale, who had also been a GM, put it. He said, 'There are only forty of fifty obvious NBA guys who can create a real edge, and the rest rely on opportunity, role, coaching, opponent, and hope that comes together with their attitude and work ethic.' This is not a science and never will be. Look at it this way. Twenty-eight teams and, what, over 300 Division I schools—the whole food chain of college basketball—passed on him."

So once again Jeremy was cut loose and asked, "What next?" A question that had become all too familiar to him.

Chapter Four: The Knicks Take a Flyer and the Game Changes

WITH THE NBA season having started late due to the lockout, and with limited practice time before a hectic, 66-game schedule was implemented, teams didn't have as much time as usual to set their rosters. The short practice time led to some early-season injuries and teams often needed an extra player on short notice. That was pretty much the reason that Jeremy found another job just three days after being cut from the Rockets. On December 27, he was claimed off waivers by the New York Knicks, only he wasn't fooling himself any longer, as tough as it was to admit.

"I know I'm competing for a backup spot," he said, "and people see me as the 12th to 15th guy on the roster. It's a numbers game."

He also admitted a bit later that he was no longer sure how long he could keep up this game of musical teams.

"There were times throughout this entire odyssey that I'd say to myself, 'If this doesn't work out . . . if this year doesn't work out . . . if this continues, I may have to draw the line somewhere.'"

New York must have taken him by surprise. Had he not spent four years at Harvard, it might have been even more difficult coming to the East Coast since he was a California kid through and through. New York was also arguably the NBA's biggest market with perhaps the most knowledgeable fans in the league. If you were good, you were cheered without reservation; but if you weren't, the fans let you know quickly. To many, Madison Square Garden continued to be a magical place, the Mecca of Basketball, even though it was now the third version and third site for the building. It was still the Garden. The problem was that in recent years the Knicks just didn't live up to expectations. In fact, the team had not won an NBA title since taking a pair, first in the 1968–1969 season, and again in 1972–1973. After that was an incredibly long drought that was continuing to the dismay of the team's many fans.

Many longtime fans still looked at that great championship ballclub as the quintessential Knicks—the teams that featured Willis Reed, Walt "Clyde" Frazier, Dave DeBusschere, Bill Bradley, Dick Barnett, and, for the second title, Earl "The Pearl" Monroe and Jerry Lucas. The Patrick Ewing-led Knicks teams came close several times in the 1990s, but never quite got to wear the crown. After that, well, it would be kind to say that the recent Knicks teams haven't measured up. Many blamed management, since the team's demise coincided with Cablevision buying the Knicks, the Rangers, and the Garden. There were coaching changes, changes at the management level, as well as a couple of nasty scandals. The once proud Knicks, in some ways, had become a laughing stock.

Finally things began to gel in the 2010–2011 season after the team acquired forward/center Amar'e Stoudemire. With some improving youngsters starting to come of age, Coach Mike D'Antoni seemed to have the kind of team he liked . . . but owner Jim Dolan wasn't satisfied. He was looking for that second superstar, and in February pulled the trigger on a deal with Denver that brought high scoring Carmelo Anthony to New York, along with veteran point guard Chauncey Billups and two other role players. To get Carmelo, the Knicks parted ways with starting point guard Raymond Felton, who was having the best season of his career, and scoring forwards Wilson Chandler and Danilo Gallinari, whom the Knicks drafted with the sixth pick of the first round in the 2008 draft. They also tossed in seven-foot center Timofey Mozgov, a big body they would miss at the center position. After the trade, the team regressed and took an early exit from the playoffs. Stoudemire and Anthony needed time to gel, some said. Others said the trade disrupted the chemistry Mike D'Antoni was seeking, and seemed to be creating, at the time of the deal.

Next came the lockout. When the season opened, Billups was gone when the Knicks used their amnesty clause on the veteran. Toney Douglas was the starting point guard with veteran Mike Bibby signed to back him up. Rookie Iman Shumpert was also given a shot at the point but seemed better suited to the off guard position. The team had also signed former All-Star point guard Baron Davis, but he was still rehabbing a back injury and was weeks away from taking the floor. When Shumpert suffered a sprained MCL injury to start off the season, the team needed some backcourt insurance. Thus, Jeremy Lin was signed.

There was one other important addition that the Knicks made during the offseason. In December, the team signed free-agent center Tyson Chandler to a four-year deal. The 7'1" Chandler was one of the league's best defensive centers and rebounders, and the season before had been a big part of the Dallas Mavericks' championship run. So it was felt that the team now had a strong front line with Chandler being sent onto the floor with Stoudemire and Anthony.

Yet the ballclub got off to a sluggish start. Coach D'Antoni couldn't settle on the rotation, and neither of the two stars— Anthony nor Stoudemire—was playing exceptionally well. Chandler was doing what was expected of him, but the team wasn't getting it done from the point. Toney Douglas didn't seem to be the answer, Bibby's best days were behind him, and there were no other options, at least not during the first few weeks. D'Antoni's offense has always been geared to having a point guard with great vision and the ability to penetrate, dish the basketball, and score when the opportunity arose. When he was coaching at Phoenix he had that guard in All-Star Steve Nash. Now, there was nothing remotely close to Nash on the Knicks.

As for Jeremy, it seemed like an old story, a videotape replay of a scenario he didn't like. He played sparingly and on January 17, made a familiar journey . . . to the D-League. He was sent to the Erie Bay Hawks, where three days later he produced a triple-double, scoring 28 points, grabbing 11 rebounds, and handing out 12 assists in a 122-113 victory over the Maine Red Claws. It was a dominating performance, and in just another three days the Knicks brought him back.

Again, he played sparingly. Then on January 28, the team learned that Davis, who was close to making his Knicks' debut, had suffered a setback in his rehab and still wasn't ready to play. At that point, the team was already looking ahead. To sign another player, they would have to cut one. Jeremy's contract wouldn't become guaranteed until February 10, so he became the logical choice. Once again he wasn't getting a chance to really show what he had. Through the Knicks' first twenty-three games he had played a total of fifty-five minutes. Worst yet, the team had an 8-15 record, the last loss coming on February 3, when the team blew a fourth-quarter lead against the Boston Celtics. Jeremy saw some time in that game, but struggled. Later that night he crashed on teammate Landry Fields's couch and was definitely discouraged.

"They told me that I was going to play against Boston, and that helped me get ready mentally," he said. "Then it didn't go that well for me and was a long night, but that's the way this business works. You're only as good as your last game, and I'm glad we have another game real quick."

That game was the next night against the equally-struggling New Jersey Nets at the Garden. Once again, D'Antoni sent Jeremy into the game during the first half. Only this time, there seemed to be a different Jeremy Lin on the floor. He started running the show, dishing the ball to teammates and scoring . . . and it didn't take long for the fans to pick up on it. The Garden was showing flashes of life that hadn't been seen in quite some time. It's said in some circles that it was Carmelo Anthony who suggested to the coach that Lin play even more in the second half. He did.

In the second half, Jeremy continued to run the show as the Knicks came from behind to win the game, 99-92. Not only had he scored a surprising 25 points on a variety of jumpers and drives, but he also grabbed five rebounds and dished out seven assists, all while outplaying the Nets' Deron Williams, considered by many as the best point guard in the league. The Garden went nuts, cheering and screaming, but did it mean that a star was born?

"I think fans love underdogs here in New York," Amar'e Stoudemire said, afterward. "They just love the underdog team or player. Also, the fans don't know much about [Jeremy], and the way he played was great for him and also for us."

Coach D'Antoni would later say, "He got lucky because we were playing so badly."

In other words, had the team been getting even competent play from a point guard, Jeremy may have well been cut before the February 10 deadline. But because of the way the season had played out, the coach almost didn't have a choice. Why not roll the dice with the kid at the end of the bench and see what comes up? With the next game against Utah, D'Antoni now had to decide whether to give Jeremy a start and really find out if he could run the show. There have always been one-game wonders, guys who suddenly find it all on a given night but have problems doing it repeatedly. Jeremy had definitely shown the ability to execute the pick-and-roll, break down defenses by penetrating into the paint, and spreading the ball around the way D'Antoni liked it.

"This is a system that is beneficial to attacking point guards," Jeremy said. "That's what I try to do."

He was also thankful that this kind of chance had finally come. "Obviously, there are times of discouragement," he said, after the game. "But like I said, God has helped me out along the way, every step of the way, giving me encouragement. There have certainly been down times for me last year and this year, but this is obviously one of the highs. I'm thankful for the opportunity."

It wasn't over yet. Sure enough, D'Antoni didn't hesitate in naming Jeremy his starting point guard for the game against Utah. Three other point guards hadn't done the job, and Baron Davis was still out. Why not give the kid a chance? At this point there was really nothing to lose. So two nights later, Jeremy was in the starting lineup against the Jazz at the Garden . . . only this time, the face of the franchise would take a hit. Stoudemire had to leave the team when his brother was tragically killed in a car accident, and Anthony had to leave the game in the first quarter with a strained groin.

As it turned out their absence didn't matter, because once the game began the capacity crowd at the Garden was treated to the Jeremy Lin show. Playing with confidence and strength, Jeremy not only didn't suffer a letdown after his great debut, but he actually played better. He brought a new energy to the team and, even with their two big stars out, everyone seemed to play with more confidence. The Knicks won, 99-88. Jeremy led the way with 28 points and eight assists, while journeyman Steve Novak came off the bench to score 19. Jared Jeffries had 13 points and eight rebounds, while Chandler had 10 points and seven caroms. It was beginning to look as if the Knicks might have a real point guard after all.

"Basketball is so much fun when you're playing on a team where people want to work together and work through tough times, overcome them, and have victories like this," Jeremy said. "This one was ugly on the last couple of plays, but this team has a lot of will."

Coach D'Antoni, who had given every point guard a shot before Jeremy, was now seeing little things beginning to happen on the floor that he hadn't seen before. He was still being cautious because it was just two games, but he was quick to talk about the attributes Jeremy was bringing to the team.

"Jeremy kind of settles everything and puts everything in perspective, and we can build on that," the coach said. "It's the second game. I don't want to get too far ahead, but I am excited. He does give us a semblance of a team that can move the ball and get good shots."

The Asian Connection

Not surprisingly, Jeremy Lin's unexpected and spectacular success sent the media into full scramble mode. Just who was this kid, and where did he come from? Questions were being asked and answered, some of them outside the realm of basketball. For example, it was quickly learned that Jeremy was one of just a few Asian American players in the history of the NBA and the first in more than a decade. Many didn't realize that a Japanese American, Wat Misaka, actually played in the NBA in 1947–1948, two seasons before African Americans were admitted to the league. But in the ensuing years, there was a kind of latent prejudice following Asian American basketball players. It stereotyped them as non-athletic, bookish, and not capable of excelling in a physical sport like basketball.

Dean Adachi, a historian and lecturer in Asian American studies, put it this way. "The most glaring stereotype to plague Asian athletes is that they are too small to succeed at the highest levels—too short for basketball, too weak for football."

Jeremy had experienced this, as well. In 2008, he told a reporter for the *San Francisco Chronicle* that "[Basketball] is a sport for white and black people. You don't get respect for being an Asian American basketball player in the U.S."

Perhaps Jeremy felt this way because he wasn't recruited out of high school despite a stellar career at Palo Alto. That was before he went undrafted by the NBA, and the statistics seemed to bear out the thesis. In 2006–2007, for example, there were nearly five thousand men playing Division I men's basketball, but only nineteen were Asian Americans. Even when the Warriors signed Jeremy to his first NBA contract there were some who felt it was just a publicity stunt by the team so they could attract the many members of the area's Asian American community.

Oliver Wang, a writer and professor of sociology at California State University at Long Beach, said immediately that Lin's emergence and inspired play would have a positive impact on other young Asian American basketball players to keep working hard on their games.

"It's difficult enough as it is to get to the NBA," Professor Wang said. "Without a few role models out there to inspire that interest, I think it makes it all the more difficult."

While the towering Yao Ming certainly helped change some attitudes about Asian athletes, he was a foreign-born player and that made a difference. Jeremy was born in the United States and grew up in ways similar to other Asian American kids. That made it much easier for them to grab onto Jeremy as a role model. So after just two outstanding games, Jeremy Lin was already, in a sense, becoming larger than life. Talk of his being a role model has already begun, even though he still had much to prove on the basketball court. It's often difficult to get a full-time job, but not so difficult to lose it. He had to continue playing well.

His second start came against the lowly Washington Wizards, a team that featured the electric John Wall at point guard, but not much else. It started slowly for Jeremy. In the first quarter he didn't score, committed two fouls, and had to leave the game for a few minutes to have a cut on his chin attended to. But in the second quarter he began to turn it on, and so did the Knicks. With Stoudemire and Anthony still missing from the lineup, it was Landry Fields, Steve Novak, and Iman Shumpert stepping up, along with Tyson Chandler. And the whole dance was being orchestrated by the play of Jeremy Lin.

The Wizards still held a slim, 64-63 lead into the third quarter before Jeremy hit a pair of free throws to give the Knicks a lead they wouldn't relinquish. Fields promptly slammed home a Lin miss, and a minute later Jeremy used a deft, crossover dribble and get past Wall into the lane. Instead of just laying the ball into the hoop, he surprised everyone by elevating high in the air for a one-handed dunk. His teammates went crazy on the bench as the Knicks iced the game with a 9-2 run.

"I actually didn't know he could dunk," Tyson Chandler said, afterward. "When it happened I kept saying, 'No, Jeremy, just lay it in.' Then, for about twenty seconds, I was thinking, 'I didn't know he could dunk.'"

When the game ended, the Knicks had a 107-93 win and Jeremy Lin had 23 points and a career best 10 assists. But that wasn't all. Chandler and Lin ran the pick-and-roll successfully all night and the big guy finished with 25 points and 11 rebounds. Hot-shooting Steve Novak had 19 points off the bench, while the rookie Shumpert scored 17 and Landry Fields chipped in with 16. It was a balanced team effort, and it was apparent that Lin's presence on the floor was making everyone around him better.

"He's unified the team," said reserve forward/center Jared Jeffries. "He's given our team a new energy. And if you look at the numbers, he's played as well as any point guard in the league over the last three games."

With all the hysteria, Coach D'Antoni didn't want to seem overly excited. He was pleased that the team had won three straight, especially since there was speculation that he was close to losing his job when the club was at 8-15. He could thank Jeremy Lin for the win streak and simply said, "He has the talent and ability to do this every night."

There were also plenty of fans at the Verizon Center in Washington rooting for the unlikely Knicks star. One Asian American held up a sign after Jeremy's dunk that read, "WHO SAYS WE CAN'T DRIVE?" Five other fans appeared in blue T-shirts with orange letters that together spelled out L-I-N-1-7, which was his jersey number. And, as a portent of things to come, there was the first play on words involving Jeremy's name. Instead of the Knicks winning, someone wrote that they were "Linning."

Linsanity Is Born

By the time the Knicks returned to the Garden to play Kobe Bryant and the Los Angeles Lakers on Friday, February 10, the entire town and sports world at large were being swept up in *Linsanity*. It would soon be defined, dictionary style, on a sports words website as the following:

Linsanity: (n) The state of excitement surrounding basketball phenom Jeremy Lin—a point guard for the New York Knicks, the NBA's first Chinese-American player, and a gift to sports headline writers everywhere.

The earliest reference online was posted on by the New York *Daily News* on February 4. That was right after Jeremy came off the bench to score 25 against the Nets in his first big game. The *News* game story carried the headline, "It's Lin-sanity!" Pretty soon the hyphen was dropped and everyone was pretty much using it, or going *Linsane*, as others said. It was the perfect term to describe what was happening at Madison Square Garden and all over New York. The whole town was infected by Linsanity as Jeremy had breathed new life into the once moribund Knicks. Instead of a death watch for Mike D'Antoni, people were gushing over how well the new point guard had fit into and was implementing D'Antoni's system. As the team prepared to meet the Lakers, some began wondering if Linsanity would continue once the two superstars—Stoudemire and Anthony—returned to action.

But first things first. Though the Lakers weren't quite the dominant team they had been in the past, they were still a formidable opponent, and Kobe Bryant continued to be one of the very best and most explosive players in the league. This game, many felt, would provide a true test of Jeremy's talents. Though it was a tough game, close throughout, and Bryant was Bryant with 34 points, no one expected the performance the Knicks got from Jeremy Lin. With the more than 19,000 fans that packed the Garden, cheering wildly, Jeremy put on a show, hitting jump shots and going to the basket with slashing ferocity. When the smoke cleared, the Knicks had their fourth-straight win, a 92-85 victory, and Jeremy came out of the game with 38 points, seven assists, four rebounds, and a pair of steals. It was his best performance to date.

"This is a once-in-a-lifetime thing," Mike D'Antoni said, after the game. "I don't know what to tell you. I have never seen it before. He got 38 points in the context of team basketball. That really says it all."

Kobe Bryant was gracious in defeat and very complimentary about the guy who had such a large hand in beating his team.

"He has been phenomenal," Bryant said. "We watched some tape on him and came up with a strategy that we thought would be effective, but he was knocking down his jump shot, penetrating, and getting around our guards. I am sure [Lin] has put in a great deal of work to always have that belief in himself. Now he has the opportunity to show it. It will be fun for the city here, obviously. Once they get Carmelo back it should be a lot of fun."

Amar'e Stoudemire, still mourning the death of his brother and away from the team, tweeted after the game, "Thanks to

Jeremy Lin and the Knicks. Y'all help me get my mind off my Bro for a few hours. Great game guys. Enjoy the win. Travel safe."

Tyson Chandler was another who continued to be amazed. "I don't think I've ever seen anybody come from the end of the bench to have that kind of impact," he said. "The way he goes about things, you would never know all of this was going on. He's the same guy who was coming here early, fighting for a ten-day contract."

But perhaps it was Jeremy's old high school coach, Pete Diepenbrock, who saw something in that game which he said was the essence of Jeremy Lin. It came as Jeremy and Kobe Bryant were running downcourt side by side early in the game. Diepenbrock saw Kobe reach out and put his hand on Lin, something he felt was a message, a pecking-order kind of thing. He describes what happened next.

"Jeremy swiped his hand away. It was like, 'Get the [bleep] away from me.' And that moment, man—that was Jeremy. He's a nice guy, but he's cut-throat."

As for Jeremy, he tried to remain calm in the center of the media-storm that was swirling around him with increased intensity. He said once again that his goal with the Knicks was simply to earn meaningful playing time.

"I really told myself this year that I wanted to be in the rotation and not the 12th to 15th guy on the team. I try to trust in God and whatever circumstances he puts me through to grow as a person. What's happened is a combination of the system, being able to fit into the system, being comfortable, building confidence, and playing on a team that is so unselfish."

When the Knicks followed up the Lakers win with a 100-98 victory over the Minnesota Timberwolves, with Jeremy scoring another 20 points to go with eight assists in the team's fifth-straight win, he received his first NBA honor. He was named the Eastern Conference Player of the Week, as if Linsanity needed yet another jumpstart. He had scored 109 points in his first four starts, the most of any NBA player since the merger of the NBA and ABA in 1976–1977. He also became the first player in NBA history to score at least 20 points and hand out seven assists in each of his first four starts. Counting the Nets game when he came off the bench to score 25, Jeremy was averaging 27.0 points and 8.0 assists since he began getting regular playing time. And as a ripple effect of the Lin ascension, it was reported by the Associated Press that shares in Madison Square Garden stock had climbed to an all-time high.

"Rangers and Knicks fans do tend to buy the stock when the teams are going well," said stock analyst David Joyce. At this point in both their seasons, the Rangers were the top seed in the East and the Knicks were the front page of every paper in tri-state area.

To Tommy Amaker, Jeremy's coach at Harvard, the success that his former star guard was having was due to a combination of factors, but none more than Jeremy Lin being prepared for it.

From the time we're young enough to understand, we know this is a country of opportunity," Amaker said. "To me, that's what is right about this story, not just [Jeremy's] heritage or his Ivy League background. This is just about opportunity, however, it's also about putting in the work to be ready when opportunity does come your way. Did he need some luck? Yeah, he needed some luck. But when he finally got some in the pros, he was ready. This kid didn't just drop from the sky. He's been grinding away his whole life. I get that he's more interesting because he's Asian American, and he's from Harvard. But when his moment arrived, he was ready for it because he's passionate and committed and he worked. And isn't that what our country's supposed to be about?

Chapter Five: Linsanity is Everywhere

THE KNICKS CONTINUED to ride high and so did Jeremy. The big win over the Lakers and then their fifth-straight over the Timberwolves put the team within two games of .500. Jeremy's sudden and unexpected emergence as the team's point guard had seemingly saved a season that looked as if it was headed nowhere. But there was still plenty of work to be done. Both Stoudemire and Anthony would be returning soon and it was paramount that the two stars mesh with their new point guard if the team were to continue its push to the playoffs. While most observers felt Jeremy was the real deal, it was almost inevitable that his play would level off and there would be some mediocre or even bad games entering the mix. When that happened, the question was how he would react, a true test for any young player.

The Knicks' next opponent was the Toronto Raptors at the Air Canada Center. Stoudemire was back and looking forward to playing with his new point guard. It was felt that Stoudemire would adjust easily, since Jeremy had shown great ability to run the pick-and-roll with his big men, and Stoudemire had mastered that with D'Antoni and Steve Nash in Phoenix. Anthony

JEREMY LIN

was the main concern, because he had a tendency to control the basketball and often slow down the offense, and that meant not running at the tempo D'Antoni liked.

Sure enough, Stoudemire played well and the team continued to excel. Unfortunately, so did the Raptors on this night, and what it came down to was an 87-87 game with 20 seconds left. The Knicks had the ball. Everyone thought D'Antoni would call a timeout to set up a last-second shot, but he decided against it. He was content to leave the ball in the hands of Jeremy Lin, who was dribbling well behind the three-point arc as time wound down. Both Stoudemire and Shumpert moved to the corners to spread the floor and take a couple of defenders with them. Jeremy showed no signs of panic. He glanced at the clock, still dribbling outside the three-point arc. He waited until the clock hit one second and then launched a three.

Swish!

The Knicks had won their sixth-straight game, 90-87. Not only had Jeremy scored 27 points and handed out 11 assists, but he had scored his team's final six points, including the dramatic game-winner. When it ended, teammates and coach couldn't say enough about their newly-discovered young star.

"You just watch and you're in awe," D'Antoni said. "He held it until five-tenths of a second left. He was pretty confident that was going in, no rebounds, no nothing. That ball was being buried."

"He continues to impress us every night," Jared Jeffries commented. "Every game he plays better, he does more and more to help us win basketball games. You can't ask any more of a kid coming into this situation."

Stoudemire, who returned to score 21 points, many off feeds from Jeremy, summed up his feelings in one short sentence: "He reminds me a lot of Steve Nash." Tyson Chandler also continued to marvel, saying, "Every single night, you don't see it coming. And then it does it again."

All the accolades, coming from every corner of the sports world, must have been a little difficult for a self-effacing, humble person like Jeremy to handle. He wasn't like so many of the me-first athletes who often referred to themselves in the third person and couldn't talk enough about their own exploits. When he arrived in Toronto with the team, there was a huge photo spread on him across the fold of the morning paper and he had to attend a news conference with more than fifty cameras and dozens of reporters. Linsanity had made its way north of the border.

"You see what he's done in arenas, and you see what happens when he's introduced during away games," said friend and teammate Landry Fields. "The crowd's going nuts. It's almost like a home game out there for us."

Yet when questioned, Jeremy always tried to defer to his team. That was the most important thing to him—always had been—and he felt that you both win and lose as a team. That was again the focus of his comments immediately after the Toronto game.

"It's not because of me," he told the press, "it's because we're coming together as a team. We started making these steps earlier but we were still losing close games and so obviously it wasn't fun. But when you win, that solves a lot of problems. We've been winning and we've been playing together. I'm just thankful that the coach and my teammates trust me with the ball at the end of the game. I like having it at the end of the game and I'm very thankful."

After their epic win in Toronto, it was back to the Garden to face the Sacramento Kings, who were coached by Keith Smart, the same Keith Smart who was coaching Golden State when Jeremy was there the year before. This one turned out to be a laugher. The Knicks had an 18 point lead at halftime and were able to coast to a 100-85 victory, their seventh in a row and the one that got them back to the .500 mark at 15-15. Jeremy even got a rest, sitting out the fourth quarter since the lead was so large. He scored just 10 points, but had a season's best 13 assists, including four lob passes in the first half that led to easy dunks, a pair each to Chandler and Fields.

Jeremy was now 6-0 as a starter and the team was 7-0 in games where he played a significant role. The hoopla about his sudden rise to prominence certainly hadn't died down. If anything, it was increasing, and he was earning every bit of it with his fine play.

"Jeremy has a great ability to run the offense," Tyson Chandler said. "Coach [D'Antoni] has the ability to make point guards great. I think Jeremy has come in and filled that role perfectly."

Against the Kings, Jeremy functioned more as a playmaker than a scorer. He had averaged 20 shots a game in the previous six, but attempted just six against the Kings, making four of them. "As a point guard, my field-goal attempts have been really high and I don't think that's necessarily good," he said. "I think it's more my job to distribute and get people in rhythm, especially when Melo comes back. My shots will go down and my assists will go up."

Asked about the media frenzy that continued to swirl around him, Jeremy said he had to downplay it. "I don't want anything to affect me or this team," was the way he put it. "Playing in New York is a big stage, and I think that's a temptation and danger to our team. We need to make sure we're sticking together and putting our egos aside. When we put our egos aside and buy into Coach D'Antoni's system we're going to win games."

One interested observer was Kings' coach Keith Smart. He knew beforehand just what he would be asked. Why didn't the Warriors see the talent in Lin the previous year?

"We did not know he could do this," Smart said, honestly and without hesitation. "And now he just so happens to be on the biggest stage and in the biggest building that every player wants to play in and he's shining in this moment. Before, he would just see the rim and fly to the rim. He would just attack the basket. But now he knows when to go and when not to go and where to go with the ball. He sees the play now. He knows how it's going to unfold on the court. He did fall into the right situation, at the right time, based on what fits his game.

"Any player needs time," Smart continued. "People say now, 'You should have played him more.' Well, we had Monta Ellis, a top five NBA scorer. Steph Curry was a runner-up for Rookie of the Year. We had Acie Law IV and Reggie Williams. And we had a young, undrafted guy who didn't know how to play in the NBA, yet."

Smart was being honest, and who's to say he wasn't right? Jeremy had worked very hard in the past year, used his D-League experience to hone his game, and simply matured. Yet, had the Knicks not been beset by injuries, he may well have been cut once again. Had that happened, he may never have gotten the chance to prove himself. It was a case of right place, right time, and a guy who was ready to step forward.

Linsanity, Good and Bad

Though the Jeremy Lin phenomenon was at a fever pitch and Linsanity seemed to be the byword everywhere, the Knicks knew that getting to .500 was a start but certainly not a finish. If they wanted to be among the elite teams in the NBA, they had to keep building and keep winning. That meant getting all the injured players healthy and continuing to make strides as a team. Despite Jeremy's on-court success, he knew that he had to keep improving and honing his game. For one thing, he was committing far too many turnovers, sometimes losing the ball in bunches—two or three times in a five or ten minute span. Taking care of the basketball is the responsibility of the point guard, and that was one area that definitely needed improvement.

Otherwise, fans waited anxiously for the high-scoring Carmelo Anthony to return, with the overriding question being would he be able to adjust his game to what the Knicks were doing with Jeremy at the point. Some said he would; other said he wouldn't—that it would be too difficult since he was used to controlling the ball and having the offense run through him. Both players said there would be no problem.

In fact, Jeremy noted that Anthony often talked to him on the bench and pointed things out during games. He said they both wanted the same thing—to win. Anthony also admitted he was bothered by stories that were already saying the Knicks might be better off without him.

"I'm a human being," he said. "Of course that bothers me. At the end of the day I can only go out there and do what I do best. I can't worry about what other people are saying. It's just their opinions, but if I said it doesn't bother me a little bit I'd be lying to you."

So everyone waited anxiously for Carmelo's return. In the meantime, Linsanity continued. Though he had just played a handful of games, Jeremy was added to the NBA's All-Star Weekend, being tabbed to play in the Rising Stars Game, which was for the best first and second year players in the league. He'd be joining best friend Landry Fields as the Knicks' representatives.

He also learned that President Barack Obama's press secretary had told the media that the president, a big basketball fan, was "very impressed" by what Jeremy had done. Linsanity had reached the White House.

"I'm very humbled and very honored," Jeremy said, upon hearing the news. "I mean, wow, the president. Nothing better than that."

But there was much more. Linsanity has spread outside the United States, especially to Taiwan and mainland China. The NBA was marketing very intensely in China, which had sent one outstanding player to the league in Yao Ming. Now there was another to root for, even though he was born in America.

Chen Yijun, a student and part-time barmaid in Taipei, the capitol of Taiwan, said, "Our bar changed the opening time from 11:00 to 9:00 AM. Recently, it has been crowded with people every day. They all cheered for Lin. Lin is the pride of both Taiwan and the mainland."

It was much the same in China where Zhu Guangbin, a journalist in South China, set up a Jeremy Lin fan club during the Knicks win streak. He posted it on a Twitter-like micro blogging service and gathered some sixty thousand followers within a week. He also planned a trip to New York, along with fifty additional Chinese fans, to deliver a batch of letters to Jeremy.

"I want to lead the first group of fans from [mainland] China to New York," Zhu said. "There are no borders in sports; the disputes over whether Lin is Chinese or Taiwanese just shows that everybody likes him."

Chinese basketball writer Su Qun, the editor-in-chief of the *Basketball Pioneers*, a twice-weekly Chinese newspaper, said that Jeremy was on the cover of four consecutive editions.

"There is no precedent for this," said Su. "That never happened before—not with Yao Ming, Kobe Bryant, or LeBron James. The first two editions, I chose him as I wanted to commemorate his feats, and make him better known to Chinese fans. Then he exceeded expectations and I had no choice but to use him on two more."

Though China considers Taiwan a breakaway province and there is no love lost between the two nations politically, basketball and sports can be a unifying force. In Taiwan alone, some four million young people play basketball regularly and more than ten million watch it on television. The numbers are even greater in China and the advent of Linsanity can only increase those numbers.

Michael Lee, deputy head of the Republic of China's Basketball Association in Taipei noted, "I now see kids here copying Lin's moves. He shows that you do not need to be so tall. He's changed everybody's perspective. Before people didn't dare to dream that they, too, could join the NBA."

Perhaps it was Wang Chenlei, a resident of Beijing, who put it best when summing of the impact Jeremy was having.

"I feel Taiwan is always part of China," Wang said. "Lin is the pride of all Chinese people. In some developed countries, there is a prejudice towards Chinese people. Lin shows that Chinese can achieve the same as people from any other continent. We are as strong as any nation."

So national pride was just another byproduct of Jeremy's sudden success. Jeff Yang, an Asian American who works at the *Wall Street Journal*, noted that Asian Americans had never seen anyone like Jeremy before, and not just in basketball, but in all sports. He referred to Jeremy's rise as a Cinderella story and said there was a fundamental difference between Jeremy and Yao Ming.

"Yao was exceptionally gifted physically. He was 7'6" and, as they said, you can't teach size," Yang explained. "He came into the league already a superstar and with gifts you can't just create with hard work. He's also Chinese, a foreign-born player who came to the United States with both a reputation and certain limitations. English wasn't his first language and he wasn't culturally part of the fabric of the United States when he first came here. Yet he was still hugely inspirational.

"But when you look at Jeremy, you're looking at somebody totally different. He's an American kid who is redefining the notion of what an all-American kid is. That, I think, is a big part of why Jeremy is such an exceptionally interesting story."

In addition, Jeremy had become a very marketable story. When he first began making headlines it was almost impossible to find an official Lin jersey with his number, 17, on it. Have no fear. Once Linsanity began, the manufacturers went into overdrive, producing and shipping the jerseys quickly. Within weeks it was the number one selling jersey of any player in the league. Fans, obviously, could not get enough of him.

At the time of Jeremy's magical run of seven-straight wins, there was a dispute between Cablevision, owners of the Knicks and the MSG network, and Time Warner cable, the company that pumped the games into thousands of homes in the metropolitan New York area. Because the two cable giants couldn't agree on a new contract, Cablevision took the MSG network off Time Warner systems. Here we go again, most fans felt. These tactics were not new and it wasn't the first time certain stations disappeared for awhile until the disputes were inevitably settled when an agreed upon amount of money changed hands. There wasn't too much protest when the Knicks were a struggling, 8-15 team, but once Linsanity began sweeping the area and the nation, the protests grew much louder and the dispute was quickly settled. Knicks games were once again available to Time Warner subscribers and most credited Jeremy Lin as being the catalyst to the settlement.

Adding Jeremy to the All-Star lineup was just another way to spread the Linsanity, and the demand for products and merchandise increased. Jeremy already had a modest contract with sports giant Nike, but toward the end of February 2012, it was announced that Nike had extended its contract with the Knicks guard and planned to release a new shoe in the Knicks' blue and orange colors and with the name "Lin" on the heel. Word is that Nike would soon debut a new promotional campaign focusing on Jeremy, and it will be only the first of what could be a succession of endorsements if Jeremy chooses to go that route. The shoe deal is also expected to help Nike increase their market in both China and Taiwan.

And as a further mark of the widespread mania over Linsanity, Jeremy Lin was featured on the cover of *Sports Illustrated* magazine . . . two weeks in a row!

For Jeremy Lin the possibilities seemed endless, just as long as he kept playing at a high level. That's always the bottom line.

The Flip Side

Nothing, of course, is perfect. There was so much made of Jeremy's ethnicity—how he was the first Asian American of Chinese or Taiwanese descent to play in the NBA—that there were bound to be some not so savory moments. It's an old story, but racial prejudice has always been a part of society, whether overt or lurking just beneath the surface. Some stereotypes about Asian athletes have already been mentioned. People just didn't feel that Asian Americans were capable of playing most contact sports. Some felt that was one reason Jeremy didn't get a basketball scholarship, went undrafted, and had to wait and wait and wait just to get a chance to play. True or not, with all the copy being written about him and all the commentary on the airwaves, and everyone trying to be clever with the puns and clichés . . . well, there was bound to be some insensitivity.

One prominent national sports columnist, known for being candid and honest in matters of race, tweeted something that was intended as a joke but contained a crude reference to Lin's anatomy, again a stereotype of Asian men. He issued an apology. Soon after, ESPN ran a headline reading "Chink in the Armor" in regard to Jeremy and the Knicks. It's an old expression where the word "chink" stands for a dent or blemish. But "Chink," of course, is also a derogatory term used to describe people of Asian descent. Again, it might have been an innocent mistake, but the headline writer was fired. ESPN also suspended a news anchor that used the same expression on the air. Jeremy seemed to take these things well. To an extent, he probably had experienced it before and, as a result, kind of expected it.

He said he didn't think anyone meant to be racist. "They've apologized, and so from my end, I don't care anymore," he said. "You have to learn to forgive, and I don't even think that was intentional."

ESPN also apologized, stating, "We again apologize, especially to Mr. Lin. His accomplishments are a source of great pride to the Asian American community, including the Asian American employees at ESPN. Through self-examination, improved editorial practices and controls, and response to constructive criticism, we will be better in the future."

The on-air reporter, Max Bretos, who was suspended by the network for thirty days, obviously used the phrase on the spur-of-the-moment and didn't intend anything racially derogatory.

"My wife is Asian," he said, "and I would never intentionally say anything to disrespect her and that community. But despite no negative intentions, the phrase was inappropriate within this context."

Boxing champion Floyd Mayweather, who has a reputation for stirring the pot, also tweeted something that made national headlines. Said Mayweather, "Jeremy Lin is a good player, but all the hype is because he is Asian. Black players do what he does every night and don't get the same praise."

Many jumped all over that one, including many African American players and others who appreciated what Jeremy had done and was continuing to do. His was a classic underdog story, and Americans have always rooted for the underdog. African Americans have certainly heard more than their share of racial slurs over the years. Think Jackie Robinson. But then again, so have Jews, Italians, Irish, and women. You name it. It comes with the territory, and once you become a public personality you can become even more of a target.

In Jeremy's case, he was intelligent enough to expect it and knew how he had to handle it. He also knew he would have to control the Linsanity to some degree, at least in the ways it would affect his time and his life. He still had a lot of basketball left. The Knicks were at .500, Anthony was coming back, and they had to make a playoff push. Jeremy also knew that, despite Linsanity, he had to keep playing at a high level if he wanted to keep his job.

Chapter Six: The Quest Continues

NOBODY'S PERFECT AND nothing lasts forever. Those are a couple of clichés that could easily apply to the Knicks' next game. Playing a less-than-mediocre New Orleans Hornets team at Madison Square Garden, the Knickerbockers never found the magic and lost, 89-85, ending the seven-game win streak and the amazing run that began when Jeremy took over the point guard position. The Hornets led from start to finish, improving their record to just 7-23.

Jeremy scored 26 points to once again lead the team, but he missed 10 of 18 shots and committed an unforgivable nine turnovers, eight of them coming in the first half. The turnovers continued to be the glaring negative in his game. His 45 turnovers in his first seven starts were the most by any player in NBA history since the league began tracking the stat in 1977–1978.

"I definitely deserved this one on my shoulders," said Jeremy, never one to make excuses. "It was just a lackluster effort on my part coming out careless with the ball. Nine turnovers is obviously never going to get it done from your primary ball handler. It is on me in terms of taking care of the ball and the game in general. Everyone gave me credit for the last seven games."

Stoudemire also scored 26, but it was a poor shooting night for the rest of the team. They hit just 4 of 24 three-point attempts. But with a game against the defending champion Dallas Mavericks looming on network television, the face of the team was about to be altered. Carmelo Anthony and Baron Davis were just about ready to play, and the team also signed shooting guard J. R. Smith, who had been playing in China due to the NBA lockout. Smith had the ability to score in bunches, especially from beyond the arc. He also had a tendency to keep shooting, even when he wasn't hitting; so it would be up to Coach D'Antoni to know when to hold 'em and know when to fold 'em when it came to Smith's playing time.

Anthony, of course, was a known quantity, one of the best pure scorers in the league. The only question was his ability to blend in with the Lin-led offense that D'Antoni favored. Anthony said he could, but wouldn't lose his identity as a player. He still felt he was the guy to take the big shot. As for Baron Davis, he was once looked upon as the team's possible backcourt savior. A former All-Star, Davis had seen his career derailed by injury and had been rehabbing a back problem. Now he, too, was almost ready.

"Jeremy is doing an excellent job," Davis said, "so me coming in and trying to give the team some spot minutes while continuing to build my condition and rehab, I think I'll only make the team better."

Against Dallas, the Knicks didn't need Anthony or Davis, because once again they received a brilliant game from Jeremy Lin, with some fine support from Steve Novak and J. R. Smith, who was making his Knicks' debut. New York would win 104-97, as Jeremy scored a game-high 28 points, adding a season's best 14 assists and five steals. Novak, playing in his first season as a Knick, had 14 points and hit four straight three-pointers early in the fourth quarter. Smith, in his Knicks' debut, hit three of his first four shots, all from beyond the arc. Though he tired late, he finished with 15 points.

But it was still Jeremy who dominated the game, even though it wasn't easy. Dallas trailed, 30-18 after the first quarter, but by the third quarter they had taken over the lead. Then, late in the quarter, Jeremy intercepted a Lamar Odom pass in the backcourt and raced in for an uncontested slam. That made it 75-72 Dallas after three. Finally, with 2:48 left in the game, Jeremy hit a huge three to put the Knicks up, 98-93, and then made a key steal in the final 30 seconds to put the game on ice. Coach D'Antoni couldn't say enough about him, starting with the way he found open teammates when he was doubled-up by the defense.

"He keeps reading it," D'Antoni said. "They double-team him every time. He still had turnovers, but the game he had was just ridiculous. You can't teach what he has inside his heart. What he has inside his heart is huge."

As for the Mavericks, they were also impressed. To try to slow Jeremy down, they put defensive ace Shawn Marion on him for much of the game. Marion, who is 6'7" and a very quick forward, was unable to put the clamps down on the young point guard.

"We were trying to put pressure on him in certain areas," Marion said. "I was able to get out there and get my hands on some passes and create problems, [but] he's talented. I give him credit. He works for it. [D'Antoni's] system is amazing, and him being able to make the pass and willing to make the pass, it's a great opportunity that opens up a lot of things for the team. For his size, he's able to make some passes that some other guards can't make."

So the word was out and respect for Jeremy was growing. The kid from nowhere was beginning to justify the tornado that was Linsanity. Now things were about to get interesting. As the Knicks prepared to host the rival Nets at the Garden, both Anthony and Davis were ready to play. Remember, it was against the Nets that Jeremy made his first extended appearance and outplayed New Jersey's All-Star guard, Deron Williams. It had only been seventeen days since that game, but to Deron Williams, the memory was as fresh as yesterday and he made the Knicks pay.

Showing all the skills that make some call him the best point guard in basketball, Williams erupted for 38 points, including a career-best eight three-pointers, as the Nets upset the Knicks, 100-92. It was a game where the Knicks as a team just couldn't find any rhythm. Anthony, who had missed seven full games, showed some rust, committing six turnovers and scoring just 11 points on 4 of 11 shooting.

"My mindset was to come in and try not to do too much . . . to try to fit in and play my game within the system and the way they've been playing the last couple of weeks. Passing the ball and trying to find the open man and making the right play. I felt good with that."

Davis had also played a little over nine minutes, hit just one three-pointer, and passed for a single assist. He, too, seemed a bit out of sync, and Jeremy could sense it.

"I think any time you have three new players—people coming back—your identity as a team is going to change with the personnel," Jeremy explained. "We are not in panic mode because it is not like people show up and you have great chemistry."

Speaking of Anthony, Lin said, "We both can make plays. We need to find a good balance. It's a little tough with no practice time. It is Day One."

One thing lost in all the hype surrounding Anthony's return was the solid play by Jeremy. He finished with 21 points and nine assists, as well as grabbing seven rebounds. In addition, he had cut the number of turnovers to three. It was a solid game despite the loss. Even Deron Williams couldn't help but praise his Knicks' counterpart.

"It's an amazing story," Williams said, "that he was going to be cut the next day, then comes out and plays the way he did against us and to keep going the way he has. Even tonight, he had a great game."

But to Jeremy, a loss was a loss, and that meant everyone had to play better, including him.

"I need to come out with more energy," he said, "and the team needs to come out with more energy. At the end of the day, that is why we lost."

On to the All-Star Break

There were two games left before the All-Star break in the truncated NBA season. The Knicks were a game under .500 at 16-17, but had obviously come a long way after their 8-15 start. Much of the credit for that run belonged to a point guard that they were about to cut. The two remaining games were on back-to-back nights, the first being at the Garden against the Atlanta Hawks. The Hawks would be without their top scorer, Joe Johnson. While this game most certainly seemed winnable, they had a bigger foe looming. The team would have to travel to Miami for the final game before the break. The Heat, featuring the explosive trio of LeBron James, Dwayne Wade, and Chris Bosh, plus a solid supporting cast, had the best record in the NBA. That would certainly be a test for the still evolving Knicks.

But first things first. Against the Hawks, the team simply took care of business. Having lost two of three to sub .500 teams (the Hornets and Nets), it was time for them to right the ship. Against the undermanned Hawks, the Knicks raced out to a big lead early. In the second quarter they had a fast break in which Jeremy took the ball straight down the middle, stopped just past the top of the key, and fed Anthony coming in from the right side for a big slam dunk. The fans roared, hoping it was a sign that the two were beginning to get a real sense of each other on the court.

Though the Knicks let up a bit in the third quarter and saw a 30-point lead whittled down to 13, they quickly regained their composure and cruised to a 99-82 victory, once again bringing their record back to .500. Coach D'Antoni, however, still saw them as a work in progress.

"We did some good things early," he said, "then we got sloppy. Then we did good things before getting sloppy again. You can see we still have a lot of guys out of sync, but we're trying to scratch the wins out."

Anthony had a better game, finishing with 15 before sitting out the fourth quarter, but Stoudemire only had seven. Jeremy finished with 17 points, nine assists, and just four turnovers.

"Right now we have a lot of scorers, so I have to get the scorers the ball where they need the ball and get people shots," he said. "I don't have to shoot as much with these guys coming back."

Baron Davis also looked better, handing out six assists before tiring. He did, however, turn the ball over five times, so the turnover problem continued to plague the team. If they hoped to have a chance against the Heat they would have to play 48 minutes of solid basketball with everyone contributing. While many looked at it as a litmus test of the team's progress, there were still 31 games left after the break, plenty of time to make the playoffs and come together as a team. But it would sure be nice if they could beat the Heat.

From the beginning, however, it looked as if the Heat were on a mission, and one of their prime targets was Jeremy Lin. Using their quickness and superior athleticism, Miami played inspired defense from the start, doubling up and trapping Jeremy, forcing him to the sides of the court and not allowing him to command the middle. The Knicks were also misfiring from the outside while the Heat scored repeatedly on fast breaks—James, Wade, Bosh, and company often slamming the ball home with authority. The game ended up a 102-88 Miami victory, but the outcome was never in doubt and wasn't even as close as the score indicated.

Jeremy finished with just eight points on 1 for 11 shooting. He had three assists and committed eight turnovers in thirty-four minutes of action. It was, by far, his poorest game since becoming an integral member of the team. And with it brought some to ask a question that had been buried for a couple of weeks: "Was Jeremy Lin for real?" and "Was he the right guy to lead the Knicks to the playoffs?"

Miami coach Erik Spoelstra indicated that his team hadn't done anything special, but that they had a world of respect for the young Knicks guard.

"I wish I could tell you that we developed a master plan," Spoelstra said. "I know that's the storyline everybody wants. But we did what we do against speed playmakers. We treated him with respect, like an impactful point guard."

Many of Jeremy's shots from the floor were short of the hoop, often a sign of dead legs or fatigue. He had been playing more minutes in two weeks than he had in a long time, dealing with the media, and the phenomenon of Linsanity in between. The team was playing its second game in two nights and had to fly to Miami right after the Atlanta game. Not taking anything away from the Heat and their outstanding players, it's a good bet that Jeremy was feeling fatigued to some degree. But, as usual, he wouldn't make excuses.

"We're a no-excuse team," Jeremy said afterward. "So fatigue didn't matter. But they did a great job of making me uncomfortable. I can't remember another game when it was just hard to take dribbles. They chased me and picked me up early and made me work for everything. They also pushed me left a lot. I think their pressure and athleticism did the job over the course of the game. All credit to them. It was certainly a learning experience for me."

Coach D'Antoni simply said, "He can't be Peter Pan every night."

Carmelo Anthony made it a point to speak with the rookie after the game. "He seemed a little bit down and we all went over to him and told him to cheer up," Anthony said. "We all have nights like this and we were playing one of the best teams, if not the best team, in the NBA. They really focused on trying to stop him. We told him, 'You're on the scouting report now,' and he managed to laugh about it."

Miami star Dwayne Wade pretty much laid out exactly what Jeremy would have to do after the All-Star break to keep improving his own game and helping the Knicks to win.

"He's done an unbelievable job," Wade said. "The big thing is that their team's winning. And that why he got [the job]; because he was helping his team win. But once you get up here, he's got to expand that stardom because now he's on everyone's radar. There's a good reason for it because he's worked hard. But he's got to continue to push, and that's what changes good players into great players."

An old axiom in sports says that as difficult as it is to get there, it's ever more difficult to stay there. Jeremy found that out just before the All-Star Game. His first seven games had been a magical ride, all victories as he mesmerized the NBA and the entire sporting world. But with the break upon them, the Knicks had lost three of their last five, and that opened the team up for some questions. Could Jeremy keep playing at the high level he had shown prior to the Miami game?

Could he and Carmelo Anthony begin working together so that Melo could resume his high-scoring ways without slowing down the rest of the team? Could Jeremy make Amar'e Stoudemire the same kind of consistent high scorer as Steve Nash had when they were teammates in Phoenix? And could newcomers J. R. Smith and Baron Davis begin producing consistently at a high level without disrupting the chemistry of the team?

"It's a little tough with no practice time," Jeremy had said, referring to the newcomers and even the returning Anthony. "You throw in J. R., throw in Baron. So like Coach said, there's going to be a little adjustment time—things to sort out, things to talk about and find exactly our identity. Obviously, you're not happy sometimes, but you go through these type of times and become a better team."

That was the obvious objective with thirty-one post-All Star games remaining. Getting to the playoffs was just step one. Jeremy and the entire team wouldn't be satisfied unless they went deep into the playoffs—as deep as possible.

"Everyone's goal is to win a championship," Jeremy said. "It's a very tough thing to do. I think we have the talent; I know we have the talent to do it."

He also admitted that the weeks on Linsanity had not always been easy. "There's been a lot of really tough times where I've just been reduced to tears," Jeremy said. "I couldn't contain my emotions just because of everything that was going on and from all the pressures and stress of the NBA season."

Chapter Seven: After the Break . . . What?

JEREMY DEPARTED FOR All-Star Weekend in Orlando with a great deal on his mind; most of which was centered on the Knicks continuing to win in the second half of the season. Though he was pretty much a last-minute addition to the Rising Stars Game, he quickly became the media focal point once he arrived. There was so much of a demand for Jeremy's time that the event organizers arranged to give him his own twenty-minute press conference; something not even accorded veteran stars. It made him feel a bit uncomfortable and it was apparent that he would rather talk about the team than himself.

"I am definitely surprised that people are still talking about Linsanity or whatever," he told the press. "I think, hopefully, as the season progresses, it will go from that to the New York Knicks. And hopefully the Knicks can win basketball games and we can make a good push after the All-Star break and people will start talking about the Knicks and not necessarily me."

There was also a great deal of speculation about how the new-look Knicks and Jeremy Lin would mesh with Carmelo Anthony. Anthony had played just a few games since returning from injury, so there still wasn't a good read on how the team would fit together. While acknowledging that Landry Fields was his best friend on the team, he surprised a lot of people by saying that Carmelo wasn't far behind.

"Carmelo, I think a lot of people have asked how he is fitting in, what is his attitude," Jeremy said. "Well, he has definitely taken me under his wing. He talks to me pretty much every timeout, gives me a lot of advice, and reminds me to keep being aggressive, to keep doing what I've been doing and that we'll learn to play off of each other."

Jeremy also admitted to constantly going to the team's veterans for advice and he told the press that they have all been extremely supportive of him.

"Two that stand out are Tyson Chandler and Jared Jeffries," he said. "Tyson is an unbelievable leader, a professional who plays the way he carries himself. He called me after we lost to the Heat just to kind of pick me up and give me words of encouragement. And Jared, the most underrated guy on our team, he is an absolute team-first guy. His defense has been unbelievable. He is always talking to me and he has been in the league for a while."

But the press conference wasn't all. Afterward, Jeremy was taken to a nearby mall to meet more than 600 Orlando fans. Many of them were wearing Lin and Linsanity apparel and stood in line for more than two hours to get his autograph. Some didn't make it since Jeremy was scheduled to be there for just an hour. The hoopla was unprecedented. In the spate of just a dozen games, Jeremy Lin had become a worldwide phenomenon. Answering question after question all weekend, he gave a good indication of where his mind was with the second half of the season looming.

"I think I belong in the Rising Stars Challenge as a young player who's finding his way in the league, trying to establish myself and help my team win games," he explained. "But I definitely don't think I belong in terms of Sunday night with the greats. I'm definitely not there. I've only played 12 games with major minutes. This is a long process. I need to make sure I'm not getting complacent and that our team continues to climb. We want to be able to get into the top half of the East and make a push in the playoffs. I definitely don't want to try to compare myself to the All-Stars and the greats."

Jeremy also admitted that the past season-and-a-half had been an emotional journey that he wouldn't easily forget. Being cut by two teams and being sent to the D-League on three occasions, including at the beginning of the current season, had taken its toll. It was obviously still very close to him and probably a source of his motivation.

"There have been a lot of really tough times where I've just been reduced to tears," he said. "I couldn't contain my emotions just because everything that was going on from all the pressures and stress of the NBA season."

As for the Knicks, he said there was just one ultimate goal. "Everyone's goal is to win a championship," he said. "It's a very difficult thing to do, but I think we have the talent. I know we have the talent to do it."

Among the many questions were those about Jeremy's future. Everyone knew he'd be a free agent at season's end, which meant he had to keep proving his worth if he wanted to remain with the Knicks.

"I try not to think about it too much," he said. "That's something that's in the future. Of course, when you're a free agent, people are going to talk about it. But that's not really on my mind now. Obviously, I love the organization and city, but right now I'm focused on this season and what I can do to help. We'll cross that bridge when the time comes. I really believe God wants me in New York now."

Jeremy also added that he loved playing in the city of New York. "In terms of platform and media, I think that's the best place to be, New York, just because they have it all," he said. "One thing I really want to do is embrace that platform and to be able to use it in the right way, and use it positively and make sure that my message and the way that I live is in a way appropriate of a role model. I'm so thankful for that."

Toward the end of one of the press conferences, someone asked if all the hoopla, especially the rock-star treatment he was getting from so many corners, might go to his head. He answered quickly and with a wide smile.

"I want to be able to be the same person ten years down the road as I am now," he said. "If I'm changing, I want you guys to be the first to let me know."

The game itself was almost an anticlimax. Perhaps because he was a late addition to the team, Jeremy played just nine minutes in the second half, scoring two points on a reverse layup, while missing three other shots. Cavs rookie guard Kyrie Irving led all scorers with 34 points, but he received not nearly the amount of attitude accorded Jeremy before and after the game. Even players on other teams were asked about Lin or made statements on their own. It showed how his story had an effect on everyone.

"It's a fairy tale," said the Suns' Steve Nash. "It's a phenomenal story because he's in the media capital of the world and he basically erupted on a Knicks team that was desperate. (You) have a desperate fan base, a desperate team and the most unlikely of saviors. And he handles it well. He's a great kid. He's very even keel and he's intelligent. It's a very interesting mix."

Rick Brunson, a Bulls' assistant coach who was once the fifteenth man on the Knicks bench years earlier, said he was impressed by Lin's mental toughness, among other things.

"He's legit," Brunson said. "That kid can play. It's one thing to get a chance, but you don't know how you will perform once it's all on you. I don't think I could have done that. Give him all the credit in the world for having the guts to prove he could do it."

And the Bulls' top assistant, Ron Adams, who coached Jeremy in the Rising Stars Challenge, remembered seeing the youngster play briefly the year before with the Warriors. "He couldn't shoot really well then," Adams said. "Now he can shoot the three really well. The first time I saw him this year I thought, this guy has got the kind of herky-jerky way of playing the game that's kind of interesting. He was able to get into cracks in the defense and so on. He found himself. It's a quintessential American success story."

But the quintessential American success story still had another half a season to play, and in the world of sports things can turn in a hurry. Yesterday's hero can quickly become today's goat. The

Knicks had 31 games to play and there were still questions about chemistry and whether Mike D'Antoni could get the most out of Stoudemire and Anthony within his system, and with Jeremy Lin playing the point. During the Knicks surge, Jeremy had averaged 23.0 points and 8.6 assists. But his early scoring burst had come with both Stoudemire and Anthony out, so he knew that would change. There just wouldn't be a need for him to shoot as much. But he'd still have to run the offense, keep everyone happy and the team winning.

The Knicks' first game after the break came at the Garden against the Cavaliers, with many of the fans wondering if Linsanity would continue. In other words, would Jeremy be able to play at a high level now that the team was healthy and finally at full strength? The game turned out to be an easy one, with the Knicks cruising to a 120-103 victory. Because there were major contributions from the second unit, led by Baron Davis and Steve Novak, Jeremy played just thirty-three minutes, scoring 19 points and handing out 13 assists, while just turning the ball over once. After the disaster at Miami, that made him happy.

"Coming off Miami, the only thing I was focused on was to make sure my approach was the same in terms of aggressiveness," he said, adding, "but to do a better job of taking care of the ball."

With Baron Davis scoring four points and adding eight assists, it was beginning to look as if the former All-Star was regaining his form and would be able to give the Knicks a formidable one-two punch at the point. The game also marked the first time since Jeremy had taken over at point guard that he played less than thirty-four minutes, and that pleased him as well. Because of the lockout, the NBA schedule was more condensed than usual and Jeremy wasn't used to playing major minutes. He had to have some concern about wearing down.

"I think thirty-three minutes is good," he said, "but it depends on the game. On back-to-back nights, it might be less than thirty-three, I don't know. Just depends on how the game is, too. If I'm feeling great, maybe forty or forty-plus, but if Baron's clicking, if the second unit is going good, it could be twenty-five or thirty. It doesn't matter too much to me."

Cleveland's rookie guard, Kyrie Irving, who had scored 34 points in the Rising Stars Challenge at All-Star Weekend, had 22 points in the game, yet committed four turnovers. He certainly hadn't outplayed Jeremy and before the game spoke about the Knick sensation.

"It's a great story," Irving said, "and he's a great player leading the Knicks to a lot of wins. He's a great point guard in the league."

While there's nothing wrong with praise, it doesn't win ballgames. More important for the Knicks was the play of Baron Davis. If he continued to get stronger and could avoid further injury, then the team would have a formidable backcourt. It was apparent that Davis wasn't ready for full-time duty and might not be for the entire year. Most felt that Jeremy would remain as the starter, but by cutting down his minutes to around thirty to thirty-five a game, there was a better chance that he wouldn't wear down from playing too many minutes in his first year of sustained action.

One thing had changed since the first half of the season, and it was something that Jeremy had predicted. During the first nine games in which Jeremy played the bulk of the time at the point, he averaged 25.0 points on 50.9 percent shooting. In the four games since Carmelo Anthony had returned, he was scoring at a 16.3 per game clip and shooting just 38.5 percent from the field. He had said he wouldn't have the need to shoot as much once Carmelo was back, but his drop in percentage was someone surprising. In addition, the team had been 8-1 in what was considered the first nine games of Linsanity. Since Anthony's return, the Knicks were just 2-2. So the questions of team chemistry still lingered.

That wasn't all. The NBA trade deadline was approaching and some thought impatient Knicks' owner James Dolan might try to pull off a deal. It was Dolan who insisted on trading for Anthony the year before over the objections of then general manager Donnie Walsh. Would Dolan try to make another move, maybe try to bring in a veteran point guard who would make sure Anthony got his share of shots? As one Eastern Conference general manager put it:

"They want to see how it all works with Lin and Carmelo. There's a lot of hype now about Lin, but they want to see how it all fits."

The one person who didn't seem to have any qualms about Lin running the show was Coach D'Antoni. Speaking of his young point guard, D'Antoni said, "He gives the guys a settling influence and an understanding of how we want to play offensively. He's spearheading that. That's the identity we want to have."

As for Jeremy, he realized that the Knicks were still in the midst of an adjustment period. Nevertheless, he felt it was working.

"I don't know how long the process is going to be," he said. "I think we're at a better understanding now and we continue to grow. It's not necessarily getting used to each other. It's finding a good balance. We've definitely made progress."

That progress would next be tested in Boston as the Knicks went up against a veteran Celtics team. It was the start of a four-game road trip, and every team going on the road wants to win the first one. The aging Celtics were a team the new-look Knicks thought they might have a chance to catch in the standings. Coming in, the 18-18 Knickerbockers were just a half game behind the 18-17 Celtics. The game was also something of a homecoming for Jeremy, who took in many games at the TD Arena during his days at Harvard. His Crimson coach, Tommy Amaker, was in the first row, and Harvard President Drew Halpin was at the game with a contingent of fifty of the school's faculty members and alumni.

Even with the large amount of supporters, the Celtics' fans showed no mercy, booing Jeremy loudly from the opening introductions. He was also booed almost every time he touched the ball and also got into early foul trouble, giving way to Baron Davis. Yet the Knicks were putting up a fight despite the fact that Celtics point guard Rajon Rondo was having a great night. Though the Knicks trailed by as many as 15 points in the second half, they rallied in the fourth quarter and the game was still up for grabs.

In what was becoming one of his better traits, Jeremy was clutch in the closing minutes. At one point he scored six straight points, including a three that cut the Celtics lead to 96-95. Carmelo Anthony then took over and scored the next six to give the Knicks a 101-100 lead with just 35.4 seconds left. A pair of Steve Novak free throws gave them a three point advantage until veteran Paul Pierce nailed a three to tie it with 4.9 seconds left. Anthony tried to win it with a last-second shot, but it glanced off the right side of the rim. The game went into overtime.

In overtime, Rondo and the Celtics took over. Anthony missed four shots and Boston moved out to a 112-107 lead with 1:30 left and brought the game home with a 115-111 final score. It was a difficult loss for the Knicks. Rondo's monster game included a triple double of 18 points, 20 assists, and a career high 17 rebounds. Jeremy, with 14 points, five assists, and six turnovers definitely was not the best point guard on the floor this night.

Taking a cue from Miami, the Celtics played Jeremy tough and hard. He was double-teamed often and forced into making bad passes . . . but he was smart enough to know what was happening.

"[I'm] definitely a target," Jeremy said after the game. "But I think that's fine, because I think we have such a well-rounded team. It's just going to take time. It's my, whatever, 11th, 12th, 13th, I don't really know. Early on, so I'm learning a lot and absorbing information right now."

He also had nothing but praise for Rondo and his great night. "He's one of the best in the league," Jeremy said. "You saw his stat line tonight. There aren't many guards, maybe no guards, who can put up something like that. We didn't do a good job of containing him and he obviously controlled the tempo of the game."

Coach D'Antoni knew his point guard was experiencing growing pains, but he still saw the advantages of letting him learn on the court and running the team.

"The thing about Jeremy, he's going to make some mistakes, and he's got a learning curve," D'Antoni said. "There's no way you can throw him in there, the first time he's ever done it, and expect it to be perfect. But he finds a way to be very positive at the end of games, so I'm comfortable going with Jeremy [in the fourth quarter]."

So now it was reality check time. The frenzy that was Linsanity, along with the winning streak, couldn't last forever. First Miami, then Boston, two top teams, and everyone could see that both Jeremy and the Knicks still needed time to put it all together . . . if they were going to make a playoff push this year. The questions remained: What would Jeremy ultimately become? A superstar or perhaps just an above average point guard? You certainly don't have to be a superstar to be effective and have a long career in the NBA, providing that you stay healthy. It was fortuitous that Jeremy happened to be sitting at the end of the Knicks' bench when a series of events occurred that gave him a chance. He also had the right coach and the right system. Also the fact that he made his mark while the teams two biggest stars were on the shelf didn't hurt. But now they were back, teams were keying on him, and the Knicks were in a fight to make the playoffs. So he would have to learn quickly if he wanted to keep his job.

Ironically, just several days after the Boston game, Madison Square Garden announced that both the Knicks and Rangers would be raising their ticket prices for the 2012–2013 season.

Garden officials said the increase was due, in part, to the reno-
vations that were taking place in the arena, giving fans larger,
more comfortable seating and improved sight lines. But many
felt the other reason was the sudden success of the Rangers,
who were currently in first place in their division, and the
hoopla caused by the ascension of Jeremy Lin. Linsanity has
not only provided some unexpected victories, but the huge
marketing effort and worldwide interest in Jeremy had given
the Garden, frankly, a cash cow. Linsanity was a moneymaker,
and in today's sporting world, it all translates to dollars and
ways of making more money. That was yet another reason
that virtually no one wanted to see Jeremy fail. They wanted
Linsanity, or at least a semblance of it, to continue.

With Baron Davis seemingly rounding into shape, many
began to speculate that Coach D'Antoni might eventually opt
to go with the veteran as his starter, perhaps sooner than later.
In his prime, Davis had been an explosive player, and while age
and injuries had taken its toll, he still had a wealth of experience to draw upon in the crucial second half of the season.
D'Antoni found himself being asked that question repeatedly
and finally spoke to it, once again reaffirming that Jeremy Lin
was his starter. He explained why:

> He's going to be good; he is good. I'm not going to mess with
> his mind right now. Sometimes he'll have great games, some-
> times not so good. But one thing I do know, HE'S a tough-
> minded kid and will find a way to win. He brought us back [in
> the fourth quarter against Boston]. He had six straight points
> and resurrected us and if it wasn't for [Paul] Pierce's shot, we
> would've won and we'd be sitting here saying he's great.

He's a marked man right now, no doubt about it. He should be. That's good. He'll learn quicker this way. He's getting experiences on how the playoffs are going to be, how it's going to be the rest of his career.

The coach then spoke to Jeremy's declining shooting percentage. "It's a lot easier to shoot the ball when you're the main option. When you have other elements to incorporate and aren't getting the same looks, it's hard. That's why the point guard position is hard. You have to make other people better and not lose your game."

So there it was again. Jeremy would have to find a way to feed the high-scoring Anthony, keep Stoudemire happy and scoring on the inside, and be ready to hit his shots when he saw the opening. Could he do it? Only time would tell . . . and that time would be coming up very soon.

The Losing Continues

After the Celtics game, the Knicks took their traveling road show to Dallas, where they would face the defending champion Mavericks. Though the Mavs had fallen off from their play of a year ago (with Tyson Chandler leaving to sign with New York), they used a formula that seemed to be working. They double-teamed Jeremy and played a physical game against him. At one point, veteran guard Jason Kidd knocked him to the court with a shot to the head and surprisingly wasn't called for a flagrant foul. In addition, Anthony seemed out of sync all night, winding up with just six points. Stoudemire finished with 26 and Jeremy had 14 to go with seven assists, but he had hit just 4 of 13 shots from the field and the Mavericks won the game, 95-85, the Knicks' fifth loss in eight games.

There had to be concern about Anthony's seeming inability to play within the D'Antoni system. Against Dallas, he had just 12 shots, compared to 18 for Stoudemire, and he failed to score in the final 3:57 of game. Carmelo was used to getting the ball and having the offense run through him. It didn't work that way in the D'Antoni system, where the point guard was the facilitator. He had success with that style in Phoenix when Steve Nash ran the show and now he was trying to duplicate it with Jeremy. It wouldn't get any easier as the next game was against the San Antonio Spurs, who were arguably playing the best basketball in the league.

Led by the trio of veterans Tim Duncan, Manu Ginobili, and speedy point guard Tony Parker, the Spurs played a cohesive team game by working together and were beating teams that relied on a more individual, freelancing type of game. The Knicks were also playing without Tyson Chandler and Jared Jeffries, both out with injuries, which would end up costing them on defense . . . big time. As with any smart team, San Antonio exploited that weakness and would end up scoring 60 points in the paint en route to an easy, 118-105 victory. The only difference was that Anthony got the ball this time and scored 27 points, but that wasn't nearly enough. Jeremy had a good game with 20 points and just a single turnover.

On this night, nothing helped. Parker torched the Knicks for 32 points, his speed allowing him into the paint time and again. Add Duncan and Ginobili's totals, and the trio scored 66 of the Spurs 118 points.

"They run everything with speed," Jeremy said after the game. "They spread us out and picked us apart. They were very patient on offense and were a tough team to guard." Then he tried to put a positive spin on things. "Tough times. We don't want to blow anything out of proportion. We haven't had everyone healthy a lot. The world's not coming to an [end]."

But what about the season? A third straight loss dropped the Knicks record to 18-21 and they were barely hanging on to the eighth and final playoff spot in the Eastern Conference. The so-called chemistry was still not there.

"It's going to happen," said Anthony after the game. "I'm not worried about that. I believe in Coach. He's smart and he has knowledge of the game. I believe in him."

Even though Anthony stuck by his words, there were many out there who didn't quite believe him. Some NBA scouts noticed that the Knicks were running fewer plays for both Anthony and Stoudemire in recent games than at any other time in the season. That, they said, was the D'Antoni way. He constantly preached ball movement over set plays and said something that had people wondering just to whom it was directed.

"If you have selfishness," he remarked, "you have trouble."

To many, coach and superstar were on a collision course. Neither seemed ready, willing, and maybe able to change their game and philosophy. In that respect, Jeremy Lin was caught in the middle, trying to run the coach's offense and keep the high-scoring Anthony happy at the same time. It was also noted that newcomer J. R. Smith and the return ing Davis both had relatively poor shooting percentages. Smith, for example, was shooting just 27.0 percent on his three-pointers, which was supposed to be his strength. Davis, still looking for the old magic, was shooting just 23.7 percent from the field and 15.0 percent from beyond the three-point arc.

One rival coach, said to know D'Antoni very well, felt that by playing ten or eleven guys every night was hurting the team. He needed a tighter rotation. Many NBA coaches essentially play eight men (unless their team is in foul trouble or the game is a blowout).

"Mike can't believe in playing ten, eleven guys and if he doesn't believe in it, how can you sell it to your team?" the rival coach said. "He knew exactly who he was going to play. It was, 'I trust them, I'm rolling with them.' Now, he's just substituting just to get guys in the game. And let's be honest. The Knicks have a few 'me' guys on that team. They need to surround the me guys with 'we' guys."

No matter whom you chose to believe, the bottom line was that things seemed to be falling apart with the playoffs in the balance. Very few people were talking about Linsanity at this point, though Jeremy continued to be one of the most popular players in the league. But his game, too, had fallen off from that wondrous two weeks when he took the team on his shoulders and created that unexpected winning streak. Now it was a matter of coach, superstar, and young point guard. What direction would each one take in the coming weeks?

Nothing brings about grumbling and speculation more than losing. Most of that speculation involved the Anthony-Lin dynamic, and whether they could play together within the system D'Antoni preferred to play. It was pointed out that the team was 11-17 in games that Anthony played and 7-4 when he had been out. Then Amar'e Stoudemire made a comparison with the team that had just beaten them, the Spurs.

"You watch San Antonio," he said. "They don't have nearly enough talent to compete with us. Our talent level, personnel, is off the charts. But what they do well is they keep the floor spaced and make sure those guys execute the plays. That's something we've got to do, keep the floor spaced and keep the ball moving and get everyone involved."

The comparison to the Spurs notwithstanding, it seemed as if Stoudemire was simply espousing D'Antoni's system and maybe taking a subtle shot at Carmelo Anthony. The criticism of Anthony's game was that it doesn't allow for constant ball movement. Once he gets the ball, the offense slows to a walk until he decides whether to take a shot or make a pass. Melo made no secret of the fact that he believed the Knicks couldn't win without the ball going through him. Many felt that his constant talking to Jeremy on the court and during timeouts was making Lin tentative and deferential. Anthony said he was simply trying to "keep [Jeremy's] confidence at a high level."

So on it went. Local papers were already referring to Mike D'Antoni as a "lame duck" coach, assuming he would be let go at season's end. Things got no better when the team traveled to Milwaukee and were beaten by the Bucks, 119-114, for their fourth loss in a row. It was a strange game. Tyson Chandler was still out with hamstring and wrist injuries, but the Knicks hit their first 11 shots only to find themselves down two at the end of the first quarter.

From there, it was a game of much offense and little defense. After hitting his first four shots, Anthony went cold and made just 3 of 14 the rest of the way. The team also faltered in the clutch. Coming back from 15 down and trailing by just a point at 114-113 with 52.7 seconds left, they simply couldn't get it done. Jeremy, however, had his best game of the road trip by far. He finished with 20 points on 8 of 14 shooting, handed out 13 assists and had four steals. In a sense, he had re-established himself as the guy to run the offense, though some would say he didn't do it against one of the NBAs elite teams. And, of course, Jeremy is all about winning. When the Knicks lose, his stats don't matter to him.

His performance also didn't convince some of the skeptics. Though he might be the Knicks' best bet, it was simply because the team lacked a first-class veteran point guard. Baron Davis only showed flashes of his old self in spurts, and with his body breaking down, he didn't seem ready to play major minutes. What neither Jeremy nor anyone else surrounding the Knicks knew was that the team was about to experience the most difficult week of the season, and it would be anyone's guess how it would play out.

Chapter Eight: It's Soap Opera Time

WHAT LAY AHEAD on the horizon had been building up for a long time. New York has always been considered one of the NBA's flagship franchises and it was a benefit to the entire league to have a strong team at the Garden. As mentioned earlier, the Knicks had become an embarrassment in recent years. There was hope when the team traded for Anthony the year before, though it seemed critics were right when they said the Knicks had given up too much and disrupted the chemistry that Coach D'Antoni was building with his young players.

The current season was looking like a videotape replay until the unlikely ascendance of Jeremy Lin, which coincided with injuries to both Anthony and Stoudemire. Linsanity not only brought the Garden back to life, but made Jeremy a national and international celebrity, which meant cash for the MSG coffers. The Lin-led winning streak didn't hurt, either. But with the return of Anthony, the team was again out of sync and losing. They looked closer than ever to a crash and burn, and something had to happen.

Jeremy wasn't immune to taking hits as well. As one NBA scout put it, "It was a perfect storm with Lin. He was perfect in

Mike D'Antoni's system. You had Carmelo Anthony out at the time. That part of their schedule was favorable. And nobody has seen him play during the summer because of the lockout. But all of that has changed now."

Many scouts and even some GMs were projecting that Jeremy would wind up somewhere between an average and an above-average starter. They felt he had to overcome some deficiencies in his game to slot into the above-average category. Those included a more reliable jump shot, cutting down on turnovers, and improved defense. And one GM asked an interesting question.

"What happens if they fire Mike [D'Antoni] and some other coach comes in who uses a more conventional [offensive] system?" the GM asked. "I want to see what Lin can do then. He's a big-time worker and he's gotten a heck of a lot better. We've all seen that. He can also score. But how much better will he get?"

With more questions arising almost daily and everyone becoming restless, it didn't help when the team went out and lost its fifth straight game, this one to Philadelphia, 106-94, before a jeering crowd at Madison Square Garden. What was even more troubling was that the team almost seemed to quit in the third quarter, playing nonchalantly while the Sixers scored 38 points on 12 of 17 shooting from the field.

"We hit a snap and we seemed to wither," was the way Coach D'Antoni put it. In other words, the team didn't seem to be keeping its intensity for the full, forty-eight minutes. Even Jeremy, who scored 14 points and had seven assists, seemed to be looking for answers.

"They're long, they're athletic," Lin said of the Sixers. "They did a good job of making us uncomfortable. We were a little sloppy. I have to keep changing things, keep changing my approach. We were a step slow on defense and I didn't take care of the ball, so they got easy run outs in transition."

It was apparent that Jeremy knew he had to change or modify his game to accommodate the changing personnel. He simply couldn't do things the same way he had during the two-week period of Linsanity. And time was getting short. The loss dropped the Knicks to 18-23 and they now trailed the second place Sixers (25-17) by 6.5 games.

The Garden fans were also not happy. At one point, they began chanting FIRE D'ANTONI, something not heard since Jeremy came off the bench to work his early magic. Anthony was booed during the introductions and periodically during the game. Yet the fans continued to cheer Jeremy, and his coach and teammates still expressed a belief in him.

"He's getting hit a lot, he's taking a beating and his body is probably banged up a little bit," said Baron Davis. "But overall, he's a fighter, has a lot of heart and we'll stick with him and he'll turn it around. [Tonight] they wore him down."

As for the coach, he said, "Jeremy has to play a certain way. The floor has to be open. He has to play with energy and he has to go. We have to get to that way and we aren't there. There are going to be some nights that are not going to be perfect but he knows how to win and he figures it out as the game goes on. He is going to be a very good point guard. This guy is going be good. He is good."

Jeremy continued to remain the optimist. After the game, he tweeted to his fans, "Stay with us Knicks nation! I'll be better and we will improve as a team. Time to turn things around."

It sure was. The losing streak was putting the playoffs and their the entire season in jeopardy. The New York press was merciless, dissecting the team from every angle, questioning the coach, the stars, and the chemistry, while declaring that Linsanity was over and even calling them a "dead team walking." There were all kinds of questions and no apparent answers. But when the team traveled to Chicago on Monday, March 12, and were beaten by the Bulls, 104-99 for their sixth straight loss, things began moving quickly.

The Knicks didn't play badly, losing to a 35-9 team by just five points, but they were outrebounded by a 56-38 count, allowing Chicago 22 offensive rebounds, which pretty much decided it . . . that, and 32 points from All-Star point guard Derrick Rose. Anthony led the Knicks with 21 points, but didn't see the ball a whole lot in the fourth quarter. Jeremy had 15 points to go with eight assists, but Rose dominated him in the second half. There really wasn't much positive coming out of the game.

Again the critics surfaced, looking to point fingers anywhere and everywhere. D'Antoni was a soft coach; Anthony and Stoudemire had out-of-control egos; Lin was in over his head and the team had no leadership. Rumors began about the team making a big trade or maybe just firing the coach. During the two week period when Linsanity became the nation's byword, none other than Magic Johnson had commented that the Knicks might well be a "tough out" come playoff time.

"It's hard to match up now," Magic had said when they were on a roll. "You don't know who to match up with now. Jeremy Lin causes so much havoc. Once he gets into the lane he's an expert at making the right play. Everybody—including Carmelo—has to adjust to Jeremy, not Jeremy adjust to everybody."

That was the opinion of perhaps the greatest point guard ever to play in the NBA. Then again, Magic knew the importance of the point guard and was thinking like one. He obviously also liked what he had seen of Jeremy Lin and felt the team had to keep the emphasis on the point . . . but that hadn't happened. The faltering Knicks were becoming New York's daily soap opera with fingers pointing, accusations, denials, and more optimism that it will all work out. With the trade deadline approaching, one local writer suggested the Knicks call the Orlando Magic and offer both Carmelo Anthony and Tyson Chandler for Orlando's disgruntled superstar center Dwight Howard. What would happen next?

• • •

ON MARCH 13 AND 14, more conflicting stories appeared. The newspapers were having a field day and Knicks fans were gobbling up every bit of information, hoping for a clue about what direction their team would take and who would help. One story said that a high-ranking official within the organization wanted to trade Anthony. The reasoning: money. Jeremy Lin's meteoric rise made him a one-man money making machine for the Garden. Ticket sales, ratings, and merchandise sales were way up since Linsanity took over the city.

Then another report came out that Anthony had expressed a desire to be traded, saying that he felt Coach D'Antoni and interim General Manager Glen Grunwald didn't trust him. It said he felt he should have more input on personnel decisions. The story also said he only wanted to remain if he were assured Coach D'Antoni wouldn't be back next year. Anthony quickly denied the report rather vigorously.

"No, no, no, no," Anthony said. "Let's nip this in the bud right now. Number one, I don't know where that came from and I'm tired of hearing it. I don't want to be traded. I don't know where that foolishness came from so let's put a cap on that and make it the last time I hear about that."

Anthony then added, "I support Mike 100 percent. We all need each other right now and this is the best time to come together and stick with one another because there's a lot of things being said out there about Mike, about myself, and it's just a bunch of nonsense right now. I want to win so bad I do everything I can to win the basketball game. If I get down, it's not on nobody else, it's on myself. At the end of the day, it's about winning basketball games. That's what it comes down to."

At least that's what it used to come down to. But in the modern sports world with millions of dollars being thrown around and athletes becoming entertainers and showman, there is often more to a situation than just winning the game. As far as Anthony was concerned, many felt he wouldn't change, that he had a scorer's mentality and had to have the ball in his hands at all times. It was also pointed out that he was shooting a career-low 40 percent from the field and that the Knicks were 2-11 in games where he took 20 or more shots. It was obvious that something had to give.

And the next day it did.

At six o'clock on Wednesday, March 14, local newscasts broke a story that shocked everyone. Mike D'Antoni had resigned as Knicks' coach, and assistant Mike Woodson was going to take over the team for the remainder of the season. And the coaching change just might see Jeremy Lin walking on eggshells again.

A New Coach; A New Direction

Though it was pretty much a given that D'Antoni was a lame duck coach and would be released at season's end, the suddenness of the news took everyone by surprise; the players, as well as the fans and media. Apparently, that Wednesday morning, D'Antoni asked to meet with team officials and owner James Dolan and asked if the team was open to trading Anthony before the 3:00 PM trade deadline the next day. When Dolan said they had no plans to make a trade, D'Antoni offered to resign. Team ownership did not try to persuade him to stay.

"This was not an event planned in any way," said owner Dolan. "We had a very honest discussion. [Mike] clearly felt it was best for the organization if he would not continue as coach of the team. He did offer to stay. But after a long discussion we agreed that it was best for the team to have a new voice and new coach."

Acting GM Glen Grunwald added, "I think he felt it was best for the organization. It was a selfless move. He felt he had done all he could and didn't see another way to positively affect the team. He felt maybe it was time for another voice and coach."

Later, the coach would say in an interview, "I absolutely resigned. I was in my car driving to shootaround and it just came to me. That's it. It's inevitable. I have to resign. We're not going anywhere. I made the decision then and there. I called Glen [Grunwald] and told him I was coming in to do it. Glen called Mr. Dolan and I met them after shootaround and told them that I was resigning."

Since D'Antoni had been present at the shootaround, the players were shocked when it was officially announced. Most fingers immediately pointed to Carmelo Anthony as the prime culprit, the reason D'Antoni had quit. Interim GM Grunwald said that wasn't the case.

"It wasn't just Carmelo," Grunwald said. "It was our whole team not playing up to where we thought it could be. Mike was as frustrated as anyone about that. That's what led him to that decision. That maybe it needs to be a new approach."

Owner Dolan tried to remain optimistic. "I want to be clear, I believe in our players," he said. "I believe in our talent. The season is not over. This team can still be the team our fans hoped it would be."

As for the players, once they got over the initial shock, they tried to rally around each other and make the situation as painless as possible. Amar'e Stoudemire said he felt the coach resigned for one reason.

"I know he tried to implement a certain system," Stoudemire said. "And everyone wasn't buying into it, so he may have been a little frustrated and felt stepping down was the best way for him. Whenever you're losing ballgames, frustration sets in. The ultimate cure to anything is to win. And at that point in time we weren't doing that."

Veteran center/forward Jared Jeffries was sorry to see the coach go. "I was disappointed," Jeffries said. "I love Coach. He's the best coach that I've had in the NBA."

Tyson Chandler defended Carmelo Anthony by saying he had become an easy scapegoat and Anthony himself claimed it wasn't of his doing.

"That was Coach's decision," he said. "I really don't know where his mind-set was at, what he thought, what he's thinking as far as his decision to step down. Ask anyone about me and Mike and he'll tell you we never had any issues. Any disagreements he had with us as a team we talked about and we went from there."

Of course, most people in the media who covered the team saw it just that way, that Anthony simply couldn't or wouldn't play in a system that moved the basketball with everything going through the point guard. When Carmelo was out with his injury, D'Antoni felt he found that point guard in Jeremy Lin and the two weeks of Linsanity seemed to prove him right. Then when both Anthony and Stoudemire returned to the lineup, it all began to fall apart.

Jeremy wouldn't allow himself to be drawn into a debate about why the coach had resigned. He tried to be positive.

"I was surprised," he said. "I know some people were talking about it and what-not, but I didn't know the reality of it. I figured after shootaround he'd definitely be here. What he did for my career, I'm not going to forget what he did for me personally. It's very emotional. I'm sad to see him go and I owe a lot to him."

That was for certain. Even Jeremy's former college coach, Tommy Amaker, felt his former star guard had found the right system and coach. "I just thought [D'Antoni's] system and style was ideal for [Jeremy]," Amaker said. "I thought it allowed him to blossom as well as he did and as early as he did."

No matter what anyone said, the deed was done and Mike D'Antoni was gone. Mike Woodson, who was brought in as an assistant coach to work on the defense, now had the job for the rest of the season. And whenever there's a new coach, change comes with it. Woodson certainly had a sound basketball pedigree. He played his college ball under the legendary Bobby Knight at Indiana and was a first round draft pick of the Knicks in 1980–1981. A 6'5" guard/forward, he wound up having a very solid eleven-year career, playing for six teams, averaging 14.0 points a game, and retiring after scoring 10,981 points.

In 2004–2005, he became the head coach of the Atlanta Hawks and inherited a team that could only manage a 13-69 record his first year. Yet in his final season of 2009–2010, Woodson led the Hawks to a 53-29 mark, which was quite a turnaround from his first season. Woodson, however, might also be considered the anti-D'Antoni. He demanded his teams play tough, hustling on defense, and preferring more of a slowdown, half-court type game on offense. Guess who that sounded tailor-made for? One Carmelo Anthony.

It was also said that Woodson was a coach who preferred veteran players. He was heard quoting his first coach, the Knicks' Red Holzman, who had led the team to their only pair of championships. According to Woodson, Holzman always said that rookies had to sit, listen, watch, and learn. Once Woodson said that, everyone began immediately wondering how that would affect Jeremy Lin's playing time. Jeremy, too, had to be thinking about it as well.

"It's going to be, including the D-League, like my sixth orseventh system in the last year and a half," he said, when asked what it would be like working under a new coach. "But it'll be all right. We're not going to change everything. Some things will be the same."

The new coach didn't have much time to prepare, since the Knicks had a game that very night. As with teams in all sports that experience a coaching change mid-season, the Knickerbockers took the court with renewed energy and played both ends of the court from start to finish, blowing out the visiting Portland Trail Blazers, 121-79.

It was a game where everyone seemed to contribute. J. R. Smith led the scoring with 23 points, while sharpshooting Steve Novak had 20, hitting six three-pointers along the way. Stoudemire had 17 and Anthony 16. In fact, it was a game in which the bench players outscored the starters, 72-49.

"It is kind of an emotional day, when you lose your head coach who I have a great amount of respect for," Woodson said. "I say thank you to Mike for giving me the opportunity to come back to New York. The [guys] stepped up, made plays at both ends of the floor. I was very impressed with how they defended and shared the ball. I think we focused a lot more. We focused on the defensive end. That is pretty much going to be the key for us no matter what."

As for Jeremy, he took just four shots in twenty-three minutes and had six points to go along with six assists and six turnovers. Some saw that as a preview of things to come, with his reduced minutes, but again Jeremy tried to stay positive.

"I think everyone was obviously very emotional," he said. "We came out with a lot of energy, more than we have had in a long time."

Despite the big win against Portland, the bulk of the stories the next day revolved around Jeremy and whether or not he would lose his starting job. The consensus seemed to be that Baron Davis would slowly move into the starting role and also probably be on the court during crunch time. Woodson's history and the things he was saying seemed to indicate that was to be the case.

"Jeremy's in a learning stage and everybody is as far as I'm concerned with me being the head coach," Woodson said. "They've got to know what I'm about and what I'm thinking, especially the point guards that play. They've got to know what I want and they've got to know the players around them and who's feeling what during the course of the game. And to be able to distribute the ball and still be able to do their thing as well."

He also added in his first long talk with the press that "when it comes to nut-cutting time and I've got a big shot, I'm going to Melo and Amar'e and guys that have done it."

With all this going on, Jeremy didn't appear to be worried. After all he had been through the past year and a half, he seemed to know how to roll with the punches. "We're going to use more post-ups," he said. "I don't know if the shot distribution is going to be any different. I think the way that we get the shots is going to be different. I'll admit I love D'Antoni's system. It was perfect for me. But I had never been in D'Antoni's system until this year. I played in another system prior to this year. So, it's like going back to what I was doing before and stuff like that."

Again time would tell, though with the compressed schedule in this lockout year, the time would come very quickly. Those who knew Woodson seemed to echo the thought that Jeremy would be losing playing time. In fact, one headline read, LINSANITY HAS LEFT THE BUILDING. Woodson was described as an old-school coach who emphasized defense, ball control, and isolation plays. He wasn't a guy who pushed the tempo, à la D'Antoni, and he held a tight leash on his point guard. The person describing Woodson then added, "Woody's inclination would not be to play [Lin]."

So the consensus seemed to be that Jeremy would lose the starting role to Baron Davis, described as a bigger, stronger, and a better defender. Toney Douglas, who didn't play much under D'Antoni, was considered a strong defender and the feeling was he could also begin seeing minutes, as could veteran Mike Bibby, who had played for Woodson in Atlanta.

Was Jeremy suddenly stuck between a rock and a hard place? Perhaps. But there was yet another factor that many hadn't considered, and normally, it wouldn't matter except that it played a major role in everything that was modern-day sports. And that was money. The sport itself might still be a game. You play, you win or you lose. But the overriding theme of organized sports was still money, and seeing how much of it everyone could make. Money was the reason for the recent NBA lockout. The individual franchises felt they weren't making enough of it. And while the Knicks certainly weren't struggling—at least off the court, Jeremy Lin had proved a huge moneymaker for the team.

It was no secret that the Knicks, like all other teams, were always looking for new sources of revenue. On the day D'Antoni resigned, the Knicks had completed a big marketing deal with Acer, making it the second Taiwanese company the Knicks were now in business with and the reason for that was obvious. Jeremy Lin. That didn't mean Mike Woodson would be forced to play him, only that his presence in a Knicks uniform had opened up a world of marketing possibilities beyond his obvious popularity and ability to sell merchandise. In a sense, he had already become an integral part of the team and the Knicks family.

But back to basketball. Two days after beating Portland, the Knicks had the tough Indiana Pacers coming into the Garden. There had been so much written and talked about regarding the coaching change and how it might affect the players that the morning of the Indiana game, Coach Woodson made it a point to speak with Jeremy. Because of some of the things that had been said repeatedly, he wanted to assure his point guard of his intentions, which he subsequently announced to the press before the game.

"Jeremy Lin is our starting point guard and Baron is backing him up, and that's the way it's going to be the rest of the season pretty much unless someone gets hurt."

So Jeremy still had his job, and the fans gave him a huge hand before the game. On the court, the Knicks were determined to continue what had started two nights earlier. Once again they played solid basketball at both ends of the court and came away with an impressive, 115-100 victory, their second straight under Mike Woodson. A three pointer by Steve Novak to start the fourth quarter gave the Knicks an 88-58 advantage, and they coasted from there with the starters sitting out a good part of the quarter.

It was a total team effort. Anthony, for example, had just 12 points in twenty-two minutes, but he hustled on defense all night and seemed to enjoy it.

"I think with the change, we had to come together as a team," Melo said. "We're locking in as a team and going after it on defense. It's kind of fun playing on the defensive end where everyone has each other's back. And this is over the last couple of days. We have everybody on the same page."

That was also a way of saying he liked the coaching change, but winning takes precedence over everything. Jeremy had 13 points and five assists, and after the game echoed the "fun" part of Anthony's statement.

"You can't describe how much fun we had during the seven-game winning streak," Jeremy said, "and that's what we're building toward."

Coach Woodson saw the kind of results he was aiming toward. "We're playing for something," he said. "We kind of fell out of the playoff picture during that stretch and they're playing with more urgency. For three and a half quarters, the defense was as good as it's been the whole year, kind of playoff-atmosphere defense."

It's no secret that defensive intensity is always turned up a notch or two during the playoffs, but Woodson wanted to see that kind of effort every night. The only down note was that Baron Davis tweaked his hamstring during the game.

"It's very frustrating," he said. "We're in a good groove. I was in a good groove finally. It seemed like the floor was spaced and I was aware what was going on out there. I had my legs right. It's just a minor setback, though."

The Streak Continues

With Davis down, the Knicks traveled to Indiana to complete the home-and-home series with the Pacers. Jeremy knew he'd be playing more minutes now as he solidified his hold on the starting point guard spot. Once again the Knicks prevailed, though this one was tougher than the 102-88 final indicated. A big, 20-6, run in the second quarter enabled the Knicks to take a 60-51 halftime lead. Jeremy drove the lane twice in the closing minutes, hitting layups each time despite the presence of Indiana's 7'2" center, Roy Hibbert.

Indiana managed to close the gap to 82-79 with eight minutes left in the final session, but Jeremy scored eight of his team's next nine points to up the lead to 11 at the 5:15 mark and the Pacers never got it below 10 after that. This time, Jeremy was the leading scorer with 19 points to go with six assists, seven rebounds, and only two turnovers in thirty-three minutes. Both Anthony and Stoudemire had 16 points in another balanced attack. But this game was Jeremy's best since the coaching change, and Mike Woodson was impressed.

"I thought Jeremy Lin was great tonight," the coach said. "He made a lot of great plays."

Jeremy was more analytical when talking about his performance. "I'm just happy we got the win," he began. "I'm learning to play in a less spread offense. A lot of stuff is still the same, but there are times when I won't have as many opportunities. I just need to be selective when I go. I think tonight was a big step for me."

He also showed his toughness as the Pacers played him rough all night. He was knocked down on one driving layup and came up a bit shaky, but scored again on the team's next possession. At yet another point he was fouled hard and flew out of bounds.

"I like it when they pound me because I go to the foul line," he quipped. With Jeremy, it continued to be team-first.

Even Carmelo Anthony seemed to be getting back on the Lin bandwagon, saying, "Lin is about winning. Lin is about this team. Lin is about doing things to help this team win. As far as the Linsanity thing goes, it's still there. That's not going nowhere."

It was all true, including the last part. At Bankers Life Fieldhouse in Indianapolis, there were several thousand obvious Lin fans at the game who cheered his every move. Many people walking the streets were also wearing various kinds of Lin apparel, and his official jersey was still the bestselling player jersey on NBA.com.

As for the team, the third straight win had brought their record to 21-24 and moved them a half game ahead of Milwaukee for the eighth and final playoff spot in the Eastern Conference. There was no doubt that Mike Woodson had them playing extremely well.

"I think this is the identity that we should have had all year," said Tyson Chandler. "Play aggressive defensively, share the ball offensively. I think that's the thing that we've been trying to get to. And for the last three games, we've been playing that way."

There was even a non-basketball Lin story hitting the papers after the second Indiana game, one that showed Linsanity was alive and well and not just among basketball fans in the United States. It was announced that Jeremy had come to an agreement on a marketing deal with the U.S. Arm of the Swedish car brand Volvo. Volvo Cars of North America, based in Rockleigh, New Jersey, send out invitations to a press conference "to announce a dynamic marketing partnership with Jeremy Lin, the popular New York Knicks point guard." It went on to say the deal would leverage "the Swedish car maker's sports heritage" and that Jeremy would "help establish the brand with younger and performance-minded customers."

The deal with Volvo was one of the first major corporate deals for Jeremy since Linsanity began. Though he had numerous offers, he was taking it slowly, not jumping on every one just to make an extra buck. His earlier deal was with Nike, which is something that many young players sign, but since his ascendance, the company had plans for a Nike-themed Jeremy Lin shoe, and that's something they only do with the most popular players.

Jeremy was certainly smart enough to know that any corporate pursuit of him, any endorsement deals and in modern-day parlance, any *branding*—which certainly included Linsanity— was directly proportionate to his performance. So his work on the court still had to be his number one priority.

The Toronto Raptors were the new-look Knicks next victim, losing to them by a convincing 106-87 margin. Again, they had a balanced and successful attack. Stoudemire led the way with 22 points and 12 rebounds, while Anthony had 17 to go with eight rebounds, five assists, and three steals. He was suddenly playing a complete game. Chandler had 17 points with two blocks, while Jeremy again orchestrated from the point with 18 points and 10 assists. Raptors coach Dwane Casey was impressed.

"They are a tenacious, different team," he said. "It's amazing, their tenacity, the way they attack."

Anthony agreed with the rival coach. "I think now we're playing at a different level, a very high level," he said. "Guys seem like they're committed on every possession, taking every possession seriously. We want to go into Philly and take on that challenge."

Or as sharpshooting Steve Novak put it. "If we play defense like this, we can beat anybody."

Coach Woodson kept pushing his team to play harder and harder. Carmelo Anthony was certainly a different kind of player than he had been under Mike D'Antoni, and once a team is winning, it usually becomes contagious. In many instances, it's when the team is losing or simply mediocre that players begin to think more about their own statistics. Right now, this Knicks were on a roll and reveling in it.

When they went into Philadelphia to face the first place Sixers, they knew it wouldn't be easy, but the Knicks' confidence was at a season's high. This one was hard-fought from the outset, but the Knicks were again outstanding on defense, holding the Sixers to just 38.7 percent shooting and they out rebounded them by a 47-39 margin.

But the team was also tired. They had to travel from Toronto to Philly and play again the next night. Tired legs usually means poor shooting and the grind seemed to be getting to Jeremy. He hit just one of his nine shots in the first half, as his jumper was looking flat because his legs weren't giving him the proper lift. When Jeremy missed his first two shots in the third quarter, Woodson replaced him with Baron Davis, playing his first game since the hamstring injury. Then a three pointer by Andre Iguodala gave the Sixers their first lead, 39-38, early in the quarter. By the time the fourth quarter began, the Sixers still had the lead.

That's when Jeremy got his second wind. He and Stoudemire did all the scoring on an 8-0 run that gave the Knicks a 71-63 advantage. Philly then closed it to two, but the Knicks wouldn't relinquish the lead. Jeremy continued to play clutch basketball in the fourth quarter. His jumper began to fall and he drove to the lane repeatedly. He then blocked a Jodie Meeks jumper with two minutes left and scored his team's final eight points, all from the foul line. In all, he scored 16 of his 18 points in the final twelve minutes as the Knicks won, 82-79, their fifth straight victory under Mike Woodson.

"It's just a credit to my teammates, how they kept the game close for me," Jeremy said. "Man, the way they defended was unbelievable."

It was also apparent that Coach Woodson now knew what his young guard could do and there was no more talk about him sitting, watching, and learning.

"He's done that all since he's become Linsanity," Woodson said. "I put the ball back in his hand at the end, and he came up with big plays."

Mike D'Antoni had called Jeremy a "winner" once Linsanity was in full bloom, and now Jeremy was showing Mike Woodson that he was a guy who could be counted on during crunch time. As for the new-look Knicks, they were beginning to look like a team that might cause some real damage come playoff time. At long last, the team seemed to be in a good place.

Chapter Nine: Trouble on the Horizon

THE NEXT STOP for the Knicks was Toronto, where they'd look to make it six in a row against the Raptors. As had been the case since Jeremy's unexpected arrival and the beginning of Linsanity, he continued to make headlines one way or another. Prior to the game, it was announced that the broadcast that night would be in three languages: English, French, and for the first time in Raptor's history, Mandarin. People of Chinese descent made up 11 percent of Toronto's population and they were still enjoying the fruits of Linsanity.

On the Knicks' previous visit, which happened to coincide with Asian American Night in Toronto, Jeremy made the last second three-pointer to win the game, and the thousands of fans who came out to see him roared with delight. It's no wonder that his second appearance would be greeted even more widely north of the border, including being broadcast in Mandarin.

Then another story broke that also showed just how far and wide Linsanity had spread. Apparently, Jeremy's lawyers had to warn shops that were selling legal medical marijuana in California to stop selling a product called "Linsanity." Most of the shops compiled with the order since they realized what they were doing wasn't legal.

"Their enthusiasm for Jeremy Lin got ahead of their understanding of the law," said Pamela Deese of the Washington, DC firm, Arent Fox.

But the marijuana shops weren't all. The craze had started when Jeremy came off the bench to lead the Knicks on their first winning streak. Now he was an integral part of their second streak, this one under Mike Woodson. Linsanity was erupting all over again. Pamela Deese said that cease-and-desist letters were written to some twenty-four entities that had applied for a trademark using the term Linsanity or even another coined phrase based on Lin's name. Most of the applicants apologized and withdrew their claim when the legal ramifications were pointed out to them.

"You can't file a trademark when there's a clear connection to someone else's name," Deese explained. "In this case, Jeremy Lin has the right to his name and related names and marks, as well as his signature, voice, and likeness. That's all part of his intellectual property."

It was also learned that Jeremy filed his own claim for the Linsanity trademark on February 13, granting him the rights to sell merchandise with the name. Why not? Though he wasn't rushing to make every last cent and still concentrating on basketball, it was the smart thing to do. If he continued to play well, Linsanity would also be alive and well, though maybe not quite with the same intensity as when it first arrived.

Since Mike Woodson had taken over the team, Jeremy's numbers had leveled off, but that was to be expected due to not only the change in offensive philosophy, but the with the return of Anthony and Stoudemire from injuries. Since the coaching change, Jeremy was averaging 14.8 points, 6.0 assists, and 4.8 rebounds. Most importantly, his turnovers had come down to a respectable 3.2 per game, and he had shown his new coach that he could be counted on not to disappear during crunch time.

"I can control what I can control," Jeremy said. "I'm not going to guess what's going to happen. The team will find a way to get everyone involved like we did with J. R. Smith when he came in. We'll use everybody at the right time."

Just before the Toronto game, a story broke that temporarily took Jeremy off the sports pages, and it was probably the only story that could have taken him off. The Denver Broncos had traded controversial quarterback Tim Tebow to the New York Jets. Like Jeremy, Tebow had come off the bench and had led the Broncos into the NFL playoffs the season before. An acknowledged and unparalleled competitor and leader, Tebow seemed to will his team to victory despite passing skills that many said were badly wanting. But like Jeremy, he always seemed at his best during crunch time. Once the Broncos signed free agent quarterback Peyton Manning, Tebow became expendable and the Jets gobbled him up to back up their incumbent first-round draft pick from 2009, Mark Sanchez.

Tebow was like Jeremy in another way as well. He was devoutly religious and often got down on one knee to pray before and after games. The way he did it became known as "Tebowing," and his arrival had set off "Tebowmania," so he already had a couple of catchphrases to compete with Linsanity.

Needless to say, Jeremy was asked almost immediately what he thought of the trade and of Tim Tebow.

"It's awesome," Jeremy said. "I'm just excited for him and to see what he does. We'll see what happens next year, but I'm excited obviously that he's going to be in New York."

When asked what advice he might give Tebow about handling the pressure of New York, Jeremy smiled and said, "Everyone gave me some advice: They said, 'Make sure not to read the papers.' But I don't want to say that to offend you guys. But that's what I've been told. I don't really read anything. I think it helps me."

Though he said he didn't have a close relationship with Tebow, he was already impressed. "I've only talked to him like once," he said. "But he's a great guy from everything I hear, and the conversation I had with him was great as well."

Having a new media star in town didn't bother Jeremy one bit. He had never asked for the celebrity status that had been thrust upon him and he knew that his main task was to help keep the Knicks' playoff hopes alive. All those extra distractions didn't faze him when he and the Knicks took the floor in Toronto looking for their sixth-straight win. They were just three games behind Philly for the Atlantic Division lead and had first place on their minds. On the other side of the coin, the team had to be tired. This would be their third game in four nights, their eighth in thirteen days. Thanks to the lockout, the NBA schedule was more compressed than ever, and on this night, the Knicks finally showed the effects of the cramped schedule. They simply didn't have it.

The Raptors shooting guard DeMar DeRozan torched the Knicks for 30 points as the Knicks trailed by 19 in the third quarter. When they opened the fourth quarter on a 7-0 run, they cut the deficit to 70-60, but only to run out of gas. Toronto kept scoring inside; on dunks and layups, and they pulled away for a 96-79 victory, ending the Knicks' five-game winning streak. The Knickerbockers shot just 37.6 percent from the field, the mark of a tired team.

Anthony continued his scoring slump with just 12 points. Stoudemire had 17, but Jeremy managed just six, missing four of his first five shots and scoring just two points in the second half. This time there would be no fourth-quarter heroics. That wasn't the only bad news. Reserve forward/center Jared Jeffries, the team's defensive specialist, was having an MRI on a sore knee that had been bothering him for nearly two months. Coach Woodson said he could be limited the rest of the season. He also said that Baron Davis, though back in action, was far from 100 percent.

"I don't think he's ever going to be 100 percent," Woodson said. "We just got to take what we get when he's out on the floor. I've got to really monitor his minutes and make sure that we don't burn him, and he's back sitting on the sideline again."

It had been suspected all along that Davis would never quite regain his former All-Star form. He always seemed one play away from another injury and that's why Woodson said he would keep a close eye on him. In a sense, it put a little more pressure on Jeremy because there was little doubt now that he would have to carry the lion's share of the load from the point.

But as the Knicks returned home to face the Detroit Pistons, no one could really know that the team was going to face yet another crisis.

. . .

LOOKING BACK AT the Detroit game, it would have to be considered a turning point in the Knicks season, though no one knew it at the time. The Pistons were not a very good team and the Knickerbockers regained their mojo, winning the game handily, 101-79. It was a balanced effort. Stoudemire had 17 points, eight rebounds, and a pair of blocks. Chandler finished with 15 and tied a season-high with 17 rebounds. Anthony finished with 15 while Jeremy had 13. That was the good news.

Then came the bad new.

Jeremy left the game with 4:47 remaining in the third quarter and didn't return. At first it was thought that he was simply resting with the Knicks comfortably in front. But after the game, word came down that Jeremy had left knee soreness, which was the reason he came out. Then, about a minute later in the third quarter, Amar'e Stoudemire also left the game with what was called a sore lower back. Both players claimed they could have returned to the game if it was close. Neither seemed overly concerned.

"I don't think there's a reason why I wouldn't play [tomorrow]," Stoudemire said. "It just got a little tight, that's all. We just took precautionary measure. It's not really a pain. It's just muscle tightness. It's really just a matter of massaging it out. There's nothing to be worried about."

Jeremy took the same approach, saying his knee soreness had developed from "over-use" and that it was "good to go."

"The second half it was a little worse than the first," he explained, elaborating a bit more. "But the guys didn't feel like there was any need to push it. But I'll be good for Monday. Doc said it'll be gone soon. Just have to stay on top of it and keep doing different exercises and getting in there to do rehab."

Coach Woodson admitted he was "more concerned about Amar'e," adding that Lin was okay and could have gone back into the game. That concern probably came from the fact that Stoudemire had pulled a back muscle (while dunking during warm-ups before Game 2) during the playoff series against the Celtics the season before and needed the entire offseason to rehab. Both players would be evaluated by the team doctors. It was certainly a concern since both had played major roles in the team's resurgence. In addition, Baron Davis was still somewhat banged up and Jared Jeffries had an inflamed right knee that would probably keep him out for at least two weeks.

The game with the Pistons was on a Saturday night. Sunday was an off day and Woodson gave the team a day to rest. On Monday, the Milwaukee Bucks were coming to town and it was a big one, since the Bucks were the team vying with the Knicks for the eighth and final playoff seed. As of Monday morning, both Lin and Stoudemire said they would be playing that night. There didn't seem to be any panic in Knickerbocker land. Jeremy simply said, "I'll be all right."

There was even a story in *The New York Times* talking about how Woodson had gone against his coaching grain by keeping Jeremy as his starting guard, fooling all those who thought he'd quickly make Baron Davis the starter. The story went on to say that not only was Lin still starting, but on most nights thriving, and that it was "a testament to [Lin's] perseverance, adaptability, and effectiveness," as well as a product of circumstance. Some scouts even noted that the Knicks were still running D'Antoni's offense about 80 percent of the time, an offense that was best with Jeremy orchestrating the show.

It was also pointed out that in the seven games since Woodson took over, Anthony was averaging just 14.0 points and 13.4 field-goal attempts in twenty-nine minutes of action. By contrast, with D'Antoni as the coach, Carmelo averaged 21.3 points and 18.3 shots in 34.3 minutes. In those same seven games since Woodson took the reins, Jeremy was averaging 13.3 points on 9.0 shots, down from 20.4 points on 15.8 shots under D'Antoni. But in all fairness, most of that came with Stoudemire and Anthony out. More to the point was that the Knicks were winning and playing with energy. If any of the starters lost time to injury, it would most likely be a devastating blow.

Then, some ninety minutes before the two teams took the floor on Monday night, the news broke. Amar'e Stoudemire was diagnosed with a bulging disk in his lower back. While surgery was not planned, the big forward was going to Florida to get a second opinion, and was declared out indefinitely.

"You don't wish it on any player," Coach Woodson said. "Especially Amar'e, who's a big part of what we do. All we can do is hope it's not as serious as it may be, and wish for a speedy recovery."

That wasn't all. It was also announced that Jeremy would miss his first game since Linsanity had been born some twenty-six games earlier. Jeremy said he felt he would play after the morning shootaround, but that the knee still felt sore and both he and the team's trainers decided to take a more cautious approach.

"It feels way better than it did two days again," Jeremy said. "But I want to make sure that when I come back, I'm 100 percent."

He also talked about the significance of Stoudemire's loss. "He's one of the leaders on this team," Jeremy said. "He's one of the voices on this team. We definitely need him back as soon as we can get him."

Jeremy certainly didn't sound like a guy who expected to be out of the lineup for long. He sat on the bench that night and watched his teammates work hard for an 89-80 victory over the Bucks. Anthony took charge and scored 28 points, while Baron Davis, forced to play more minutes without Jeremy, had 13 points and seven assists, but also added nine turnovers.

"It was an ugly game," Coach Woodson said, "but the second half was tremendous defensively."

The only good news was that the victory gave the Knicks seven of eight games under Woodson and they now led the Bucks by 2.5 games for the final playoff spot. But the news before the next game against the Orlando Magic was all about the injuries. The second opinion sought by Stoudemire confirmed the bulging disk and he would need to undergo non-surgical treatment. With 16 games left to the regular season, word was that the Knicks hoped to get him back for the first round of the playoffs. Any time sooner would be a bonus.

Dr. Wellington Hsu, an orthopedic surgeon at Northwestern Memorial Hospital in Chicago, is a sports medicine specialist who said that a common procedure for treating bulging disks in pro athletes was an epidural steroid injection, as well as oral anti-inflammatory medication. If the treatment worked quickly, it was thought that Stoudemire could be back within ten days, but Dr. Hsu said that would not be his choice. Though he hadn't treated Stoudemire personally, he said that back-strengthening and rehab exercises to increase power in the core over a four-week period is the best course of treatment because it would be the best chance that Amar'e could avoid reinjuring his back.

"He has to demonstrate a full range of motion in his back without any pain," Dr. Hsu said. He also added that a bulging disk doesn't go away unless the athlete opts for surgery. "That would be a very reasonable option for the offseason," he added.

As it was now apparent that Stoudemire would be likely gone for the remainder of the regular season, everyone's attention turned to Jeremy. Could the team really afford to lose two starters? With the Orlando Magic looming, Jeremy was listed as questionable, but he reiterated that he wouldn't return until he was fully recovered. He also said that the knee had begun giving him pain the past Friday in Toronto and that the pain was the reason had left the game against the Pistons.

"I'm just making sure that I'm 100 percent pain free before I come back," he said. "Just being cautious. Just being sure I don't have to deal with this again sometime down the road."

Will He or Won't He?

While there was no question about Amar'e Stoudemire's injury, the status of Jeremy remained up in the air. It still wasn't announced whether or not he would play against the Magic. Yet the only thing anyone would say is that he had knee soreness. But because he was Jeremy Lin, he made some news that had nothing to do with the knee or the next game.

According to a story in *Newsday*, a local New York paper, Jeremy had met quietly with Anthony Federico, the former ESPN editor who had lost his job when he inadvertently published the headline, "Chink in the Armor," a month earlier. The headline ran when the Knicks had finally lost a game after the magic of Linsanity had begun. The headline was changed after just thirty-five minutes and when the network issued an apology, it also announced that Federico had been terminated. At the time, he said:

"This had nothing to do with me being cute or punny. I'm so sorry that I offended people. I'm so sorry if I offended Jeremy."

After losing his job, Federico issued another long apology on Twitter, again saying it was an honest mistake, and he also referred to the fact that he and Jeremy both shared the Christian faith. At that time, Federico listed an email address and a member of Lin's family had reached out offering to arrange a time for Jeremy to meet with him. After the meeting, Federico couldn't say enough about Jeremy.

"The fact that he took the time to meet with me in his insanely busy schedule, well, he's just a wonderful, humble person," Federico said. He also said that their conversation was mostly geared to ideas of reconciliation and their shared faith.

Jeremy's willingness to meet with Federico was described as "classy," and earned him even more praise from the press and media. Of course, no story about Jeremy at this point could be written without conjecture about his knee. At game time with the Magic, Jeremy was again out of the lineup. Official word was that he still was in pain. Without their two starters, the Knicks went out and trimmed the Magic handily, 108-86, bringing them a game above .500 at 26-25. It was the first time in two months that they'd been over .500, since they had a 6-5 record at the beginning of the season. Anthony and rookie Iman Shumpert led the way with 25 points each. The Knicks had outscored the Magic, 32-12, in the second quarter and continued to blow them out in the third.

When Jeremy missed their next game, a 100-90 loss to the Atlanta Hawks, even the newspapers began calling his absence a "building mystery." One reporter said that Jeremy had poked his head out of a door to the Knicks' training room and when he saw several reporters in the hallway, quickly closed it and stayed inside. He obviously didn't want to talk about his knee or speculate on a possible return. Those continuing to wonder about his health had the feeling it was just wear and tear from Jeremy logging so many minutes after hardly playing at all at the beginning of the season.

Even though Jeremy was out, Coach Woodson said the Knicks were still being cautious with Baron Davis's increased minutes. The coach was then asked if Jeremy had an MRI for what he termed "a bum knee."

"I think he's already had one," Woodson said. "Again, I think he's okay. But we'll take it one day at a time and see what's going to happen. He was out shooting today. When he tells me he is ready to go, that's going to put a smile on my face."

A day later, the coach seemed a bit more pessimistic, saying he did not know when or if both Amar'e and Jeremy would return. Stoudemire had an epidural injection for his bulging disk and they were hoping for the best. But it was the "when" and "if" with regard to Jeremy that set off a feeding frenzy amongst the media. The Knicks' next game was against the Cavaliers and there was no word whether Jeremy would be able to go out there.

While the injury was still referred to as knee soreness, a team source supposedly said there might be some loose cartilage that would need to be scoped after the season. Woodson also reiterated that Jeremy had an MRI, but that he didn't know the results. The official word continued to be that Jeremy was receiving treatment and that the team was optimistic that he would be good enough to play soon and go right through the playoffs.

But it was the Knicks' ambivalence and secrecy about the severity of the injury that were raising red flags. Always one of the most accessible of athletes, Jeremy was suddenly going out of his way to avoid talking to the press. Reporters kept referring back to Woodson's "when" and "if" statement, wondering if he knew more than he was letting on or had let something slip out. One thing was certain: This couldn't go on much longer. There had to be a resolution . . . and soon.

After Jeremy was declared out of the Cavaliers game, a person close to him gave the press a "maybe" in regard to Tuesday's game at Indiana. Then another source claimed that the earliest Jeremy would return would be the following Thursday against Orlando. No one seemed to have a straight answer. Some said that if he returned he'd have to be able to play through pain. Others speculated that the original Linsanity run spurred defenses to play him tight and hard, and the physical defense, which saw him roughed up and knocked down repeatedly, had taken a toll on a knee not used to all the contact.

"He mixes it up," Woodson admitted. "When you're a point guard, you're getting touched by big guys on the pick and rolls. It's tough. He's pretty good at getting to the bucket and finishing, and taking the blow and drawing fouls. It's a lot of wear and tear on the body."

Then, finally, the news broke . . . and took a lot of people by surprise.

The announcement came on Saturday, March 31, just prior to the Knicks game against the Cavaliers. Jeremy apparently was found to have a small meniscus tear in his knee that would require arthroscopic surgery that would keep him out for at least six weeks. That meant he would miss the remainder of the regular season and the first round of the playoffs. If the team was some-how able to get through to the second round, there was a chance he would be able to play. The announcement came a week after he first complained of soreness in the knee on March 24, when he came out of the game against Detroit in the third quarter. The injury was called a small but chronic tear in the meniscus; chronic meaning the injury had been present for some time.

Both Jeremy and the team had hoped to delay surgery until after the season, but they said his knee did not respond sufficiently to treatment over the course of the week. He tested it one final time on Saturday morning, and then decided on immediate surgery.

"I can't really do much, can't really cut or jump," Jeremy said, at a hastily-arranged press conference. "So it's pretty clear that I won't be able to help the team unless I get this fixed right now. It's disappointing for me. It's hard to watch the games. And I want to be out there, obviously, more than anything, to help the team."

Though Jeremy would be a restricted free agent after the season, meaning no team would be allowed to offer more than the average salary of about $5 million, with the Knicks having the right to match any offer, Jeremy quickly indicated that his first choice would be to remain in New York.

"It's been an unbelievable journey," he said. "I would love to keep this team together as long as we can, everybody, top to bottom."

Once again, Jeremy was being the consummate professional, supporting each and every teammate, even on a flawed team. But there were two undeniable facts. If the Knicks were indeed flawed, they would now be even more flawed with Jeremy out of the lineup. And the second part of the equation was that the feel good Cinderella story that was Linsanity was now over, at least for the remainder of the regular season. For a twenty-three-year-old undrafted Asian American Harvard graduate to come from nowhere to lead an NBA team on an eye-catching winning streak was the story of the year, especially around New York. Though, with a coaching change and seemingly disgruntled superstar, the story had become more soap opera than magical. But now part of it was at best . . . on hold.

Jeremy also revealed that the tear had been diagnosed on Monday night, but the decision to opt for surgery wasn't made until Saturday. "Our goal was to give it five to seven days to see how it reacts and see if I can play on it the rest of the season,"

Jeremy said, again. "I knew I had to have surgery at some point, whether it was now or after the end of the season. We did rehab it all day (for a week). We did everything we could. That's why I couldn't talk about the injury until now.

"It's a six-week rehab process," Jeremy continued. "I can heal fast. I can come back as soon as possible and contribute this season, hopefully. It's disappointing for me, hard to watch the games. I just want to be out there more than anything else."

Mike Woodson, who at first seemed to dismiss Jeremy as an inexperienced rookie, had obviously come to respect him during the short time he coached him. He kind of said it all in one short sentence.

"This is a big blow for us."

Despite the fact that Jeremy had to acclimate to a new coach, the returning superstars, and wasn't putting up quite the gaudy numbers of Linsanity, he was still one of the most popular players in New York and throughout the league. That's how compelling his story had become. Obviously, Jeremy didn't want it to end like this, and that's why he and the trainers decided to try one week of intensive therapy and why they didn't make a definite decision to opt for surgery until Saturday morning. Had his knee responded to the point where he felt he could play and contribute and wouldn't do further damage, he might have tried to tough it out for the rest of the season. But it hadn't, and he opted for the surgery.

The Knicks without Linsanity

To the rest of the Knicks, it didn't really matter when the announcement was made to the fans and media. The bottom line to them was that they had lost their starting point guard, a player who had earned everyone's respect with his hard-nosed play and toughness. On the night Jeremy announced that he'd need surgery, the Knicks went out and beat the Cavs, 91-75. But after the game, there wasn't the usual joy in the winning locker room. Lin's sobering news left everyone more or less downcast.

"It's tough," Carmelo Anthony said, when asked about Lin's absence. "I really didn't know until today. For him to be out six weeks and to have surgery, that's most important. We want him to take care of that. Basketball stuff comes second."

Said Tyson Chandler, "You feel for your teammate. You never want to see someone go through surgery, especially someone who was playing so well. We'll be with him, and we just have to keep the boat floating until he gets back."

Chandler wasn't concerned about Jeremy's ultimate recovery. "He's so young," he said. "I think he'll be fine. It's not a veteran who has played a lot. But I know what he was going through. He's so tough. For him not to play, you know he is hurting."

There was a time just a few weeks earlier when the Knicks were considered a deep team, with two full units getting solid playing time. Now Stoudemire, Jared Jeffries, and Jeremy were all on the shelf. Anthony and Chandler were playing with minor bumps and bruises and there was already concern that Baron Davis could break down since he was now going to be playing more minutes each night. But the Knicks weren't the only team beset by injuries, and Cavaliers coach Byron Scott felt he knew why.

"You've got a lot of games compiled in a short period of time and these guys didn't have the type of training camp they're used to having," Scott said, referring to the NBA lockout. "Your body and your mind are programmed to go from July to September getting ready for training camp. A lot of guys probably shut it down in October because there was no end in sight to the lockout. Then they had a week to start to get prepared again and now I think it's starting to take its toll on a lot of players."

Jeremy's sudden jump from end-of-the-bench scrub to starter certainly brought sudden wear and tear to his body, but there was still some hope he might return sooner than six weeks. Dr. Wellington Hsu, the orthopedic surgeon who had commented on Amar'e Stoudemire's bulging disk, also explained Jeremy's injury more thoroughly, saying that the key to recovery was the level of arthritis that surgeons found when they went in to repair the meniscus. However, he did warn that because the tear was described as "chronic," by definition some arthritis would exist.

"If they don't see anything else wrong in surgery, just see the tear, typically you can get back in the NFL in two to four weeks and I've seen NBA players get back within that period," Dr. Hsu explained. "But the more arthritis, the harder a time he'll have getting back as quickly as possible."

The doctor also saw Jeremy's statements that he couldn't really cut or jump when he tested the knee after a week of therapy. "If he had a high level of function before surgery, it would take less time," Hsu said, "but since he was really hurting and can't cut at all, maybe it takes him a little longer." Dr. Hsu also felt that Jeremy probably had the problem for at least six months and that his sudden increase in playing time in a compressed schedule only made it worse.

"Not only was [Jeremy] being played thirty-eight to forty minutes a night after being a fourth stringer, there was also no time between games because of the lockout."

So while Jeremy had to face surgery, his teammates had to face the rest of the season without him, and possibly without Amar'e as well. The other concern was Baron Davis. Davis, like any other proud athlete, felt he would be fine. But in his four starts since Jeremy's departure, Davis had averaged 8.5 points, 5.5 assists, and 4.0 turnovers a game, and just shooting 33.3 percent from the field. One observer said "his legs look heavy and his jumps shot flat. He rarely gets to the basket or draws a foul." These, of course, were all things that Jeremy was doing before his injury.

"I'm definitely not happy with where my game is," Davis admitted. "I definitely know that I can get back to my old self and doing the things that I've been capable of doing. I may have lost a lot of athleticism, but I can still pass the ball well and run a team, and that's where my focus is right now."

The Knicks were doing the best they could to limit Davis's minutes. He had averaged just 16.7 minutes in 15 games as Jeremy's backup since returning to the lineup. As a starter, he was averaging 28.0 minutes with a high of 34 in the March 26 win over the Bucks. Coach Woodson was well aware that Baron would probably not be a full strength the rest of the season.

"I can't play him thirty minutes," the coach said. "You just can't do it, because I just don't feel like he'll have much left. It might take him a day or two to recover."

The alternatives weren't at all that appealing. Toney Douglas had been the point guard early in the season and was pretty much benched when Jeremy came from out of nowhere. Mike

Bibby was thirty-three-years-old and his best days were far behind him. Rookie Iman Shumpert, a terrific defensive player, got a short try at running the point, but it was apparent that he was better suited as a shooting guard. So Coach Woodson would have to mix and match, make the best of a situation that was far from optimal. Yes, the coach, the player, the fans, and the team as a whole would definitely miss Jeremy Lin.

Jeremy had his surgery on Monday, April 1, and by all reports it went well with no complications. Now the recovery period would begin . . . immediately. The Knicks, at 27-26, led the 25-28 Bucks by two games for the final playoff spot. What seemed like a lock just two weeks earlier was now an uncertain situation, mainly because of the injuries. There were now 13 games remaining and they would be played in just twenty-six days, a difficult schedule for even healthy players. That's what the lockout had caused.

The first game after Jeremy's surgery showed just how much he was missed. The Knicks had a 17 point lead against Indiana late in the third quarter and suddenly collapsed, being out-scored 40-17 in the final quarter and losing to the Pacers, 112-104. Anthony finished with a season-high 39 points, but that wasn't enough. It also indicated that the team was revert-ing to a half-court offense and going through their leading scorer. Davis had a shaky game, hitting just 2 of 8 shots from the field and totaling just three assists in nearly thirty minutes of action. The Knicks also slackened on the defensive end, los-ing the edge they had come with the appointment of Mike Woodson as head coach.

Now the team was back to .500 at 27-27. With a dozen games remaining and a playoff berth at stake, it now really was crunch time.

Chapter Ten: The Homestretch

TWO DAYS AFTER losing to Indiana, the Knicks rolled into Orlando to face the Magic. They came in at a good time, since internal problems had made Orlando a mediocre team. Star center Dwight Howard had alternately lobbied for a trade as opposed to a long-term deal at several points in the season, seemingly going back and forth and then expressing his displeasure with Coach Stan Van Gundy, who would end up losing his job after the season. So the once formidable team was in disarray, and the Knicks took advantage, winning the game, 96-80.

Anthony had 19 in this one, as Chandler played tough, physical defense on Dwight Howard, holding him scoreless in the first half. Chandler also had 12 points and 12 rebounds. J. R. Smith came out of a brief funk and scored 15 points, 13 of them in the first half. On the other side of the coin, Baron Davis didn't play much because of his knee and hamstring tweaks, but the seldom-used Toney Douglas came off the bench to score 15 points. The victory made the Knicks 5-2 in the seven games since both Stoudemire and Lin were injured. The better they played now the better chance of getting their two injured players back down the road, even if it was in the playoffs.

The same day the Knicks defeated the Magic, Jeremy spoke to the press for the first time. The main question was and would continue to be when he thought he could return. At this point, he didn't sound too optimistic about the first round of the playoffs. He said that he wouldn't rush back and that he was only doing some stationary bike work, as fluid on his knee still prevented him from running. When asked about the first game of the playoffs, Jeremy just shook his head, saying,

> I think if something goes really well, but I probably wouldn't be able to get there. It depends how far it goes. I obviously want to come back to 100 percent and then come back and see what I can do. By then, it would be a different team with chemistry. So it gets sticky, too. We haven't set a best case yet. We're happy with the way things have gone. It's hard to tell because there's so much fluid.

Jeremy said that straight ahead running wouldn't be the issue. "The cutting and jumping, that's going to be the tricky part."

It was pretty apparent that Jeremy wouldn't rush his rehab. He knew he wouldn't really be helping the team if he wasn't at full strength and he certainly didn't want to risk re-injuring his knee. So there would be no quick returns; no miracles that would suddenly see number 17 back on the court early. The Knicks would have to make their playoff push without him and they went back to work.

Their next opponent would be the very tough Chicago Bulls. This one quickly became the Carmelo Anthony show. Anthony thrilled the Garden crowd with a 43-point performance as the Knicks won, 100-99, in overtime. Not only did Melo hit a game tying basket with 11.2 seconds left in regulation, but he also nailed the game-winner with just 8.2 seconds remaining in the first overtime. He was supported by a yeoman effort from Tyson Chandler, who grabbed 16 rebounds with 10 of them at the offensive end. The win gave the Knicks a 29-27 record and a one-game lead on the Bucks for the final playoff spot. But they had also pulled even with the slumping Sixers for the seventh seed as the Boston Celtics now led the division.

It was a quick turnaround to Chicago for the second game of a home-and-home series with the Bulls, and this time they were the ones who prevailed with a 96-86 final score. The Bulls had won it without their MVP guard, Derrick Rose, who sprained his ankle the night before. But the New York point guards couldn't take advantage of Rose's absence, which ended up being the deciding factor. Anthony had 29 points and Chandler had another 15 rebound game; but as one beat writer noted, "The continued absences of point guard Jeremy Lin and Amar'e Stoudemire was deeply felt." Once again the Knicks were tied with the Bucks and were set with a showdown meeting the following night in Milwaukee.

Against the Bucks, it became painfully apparent that Baron Davis just wasn't physically ready to carry a full load at the point. The veteran was now battling knee, neck, and hamstring injuries, and had to be pulled in the third quarter with just five points and three assists (including five turnovers) in nineteen minutes. It could have been a disaster, had rookie Iman Shumpert not come to the rescue.

The 6'5" Shumpert had failed an early season audition at the point, though he had proven to be a solid shooting guard, and was perhaps the Knicks' best perimeter defender. On this night, he not only produced 16 points, six rebounds, and five assists, but he only committed one turnover in forty-two minutes. In addition, he did a great defensive job on the Bucks' speedy guards Brandon Jennings and Monta Ellis. Add a 32-point effort from Carmelo Anthony and the Knicks had a big, 111-107, victory.

"I just knew we needed this win," Shumpert said after the game. "I was just going to go hard every play. We understand, the guards on the team, that our roles are going to switch at any given time, depending on who is who. Everything is about winning now."

Coach Woodson also expressed his satisfaction with the rookie. "I feel comfortable with [Shumpert] handing the basketball and getting us into things," Woodson said. "It makes us bigger and we can switch more defensively."

Lin's injury had obviously forced Woodson to become more creative with his personnel. There was no set formula. It was as if the Knicks were simply going night to night, and so far it seemed to be working. In addition, Anthony had completely shaken his shooting slump and had returned to being one of the best pure scorers in the league.

The following game ended in a laugher, as the team easily defeated the Washington Wizards, 103-65. This time they didn't need Anthony to have a huge game. He wound up with 18 points in just twenty-seven minutes. The big surprise was Baron Davis, shaking off the affects of his injuries on his thirty-third birthday to score a season-high 18 points, including 4 of 5 from three-point land. And the good news for the now

31-28 Knicks was that the 76ers had lost to the Nets, putting the Knicks into the seventh playoff slot.

Next up was LeBron James, Dwayne Wade, Chris Bosh, and the Miami Heat. They would be coming into the Garden in what might be a first-round playoff preview. Since taking over the team, Woodson had coached the Knicks to a 9-0 record at the Garden and 13-4 mark overall. He felt the home court could give his team an advantage.

"I'm hoping so, absolutely," he said. "We've been playing well here at home. It's going to take a great forty-eight minute ballgame. [The Heat] are a great team. I thought they dominated us when we were there. The games were fairly close in stretches, but their defense overshadowed our defense. That was the difference. [Now] we're a lot better defensively."

Unlike their last meeting, the Knicks showed up against the Heat, but once again, they didn't have the finishing power they needed. With 8:01 remaining in the fourth quarter, New York held a 79-75 lead over LeBron James and company, only to see them fritter it away and lose, 93-85.

"I don't know what happened. It was a blur. I just happened so fast," said Carmelo Anthony, who had 42 points in the loss.

For coach Woodson, it was a matter of his team not reacting quickly enough. "I thought our pace was so slow. We got to get the ball out quicker and get in our offense," he said. "In the third quarter we relied on our jump shot and did not get to the free throw line."

It didn't help that Chandler banged his knee in the third quarter and limped home. Iman Shumpert was playing with a slight ankle sprain and was not at full strength either. He held his own defensively, mostly against Wade, but didn't shoot well and scored just three points. J. R. Smith helped keep the Knicks in the game with 16 points. At 31-29, the team was back in the eighth and final playoff spot, but trailed the seventh place Sixers by just half a game. Neither spot augured well. If the Knicks finished eighth, they would probably play the Bulls, and if they managed to take seventh, it would be the Heat.

Next up was the first-place Celtics at MSG. Though just four games separated the two teams, it was a stretch to think the Knicks could take the division. It had already been a season of highs and lows for the team: unexpected injuries, some dissension, and a coaching change. And as one local writer reminded everyone, "They began the season without a point guard, then found a surprisingly good one, only to lose him to a knee injury."

Though the team was hanging in there, they certainly missed what Jeremy had brought to the table. He might not have been the instant superstar that some made him out to be during the stretch of Linsanity, but he had played extremely well, showed a penchant for coming up big at crunch time, and was tough as nails. It was obvious that the team missed him. Anthony was again the primary—and sometimes only—scoring option. Without Jeremy to distribute the basketball, the offense had become one-dimensional, spotty, and often looked out of rhythm.

Though the Knicks were 13-5 since the six-game losing streak that led to Mike D'Antoni's resignation, it was pointed out that they had little luck against the elite teams of the Eastern Conference. They were a combined 2-8 against division leaders

Miami, Chicago, and Boston, having beaten the Celtics and Bulls one time each at home. That, too, was an ominous sign for the upcoming playoffs. Only on this night at the Garden, the Knicks were on fire. The final score was 118-110, and when the smoke cleared, the Knickerbockers had hit 19 three-pointers.

Anthony led the way with the second triple-double of his career, scoring 36 points to go with 12 rebounds and 10 assists. But it was the reserves that really brought the crowd to life with their long-range shooting. Steve Novak and J. R. Smith both scored 25 points coming off the bench and helped the team to a season-best 72-point first half. To make the victory even sweeter, Tyson Chandler dominated inside and scored 20 points of his own. But it was Novak and Smith who lit up the crowd. Novak hit 8 of 10 from long range, while Smith went 7 of 10.

"The fans really get into it," Smith said. "You can feel the roar. It's a great feeling. When you are playing at home, it is great, period. When you play here at the Garden, it's indescribable."

It was a game to remember as the Knicks' bench outscored Boston's by an incredible 57-2 margin. "That's been our M.O. for awhile," Steve Novak said after the game. "To have the bench come in and give us a boost, that's when we're at our best. That's a pretty big number there (referring to the 55-point bench margin)."

If nothing else, the game may have been an indication of what the Knicks would have to do to have any success in the playoffs, especially if they didn't have Stoudemire and Lin back. Chandler would have to dominate inside while Anthony scored from all over the court. At the same time,

Novak and Smith would have to shoot the eyes out of the hoop from beyond the arc. It couldn't happen every night. Nothing does. But to win without a solid point guard and second inside force, they would simply have to outshoot their opponents.

The next game was a wire-to-wire victory over the Nets, 104-95. Anthony seemed to score at will early, netting 21 points before the end of the first quarter. It was 64-47 at the half, and the Knicks cruised from there. The win brought the team's record to 33-29 and moved them three and a half games ahead of the Bucks for the eighth playoff spot. That wasn't all. They were now a game and a half in front of the Sixers for the seventh seed and now just needed one more victory to clinch a playoff berth.

In between games, a story broke that reminded Knicks and New York sports fans not only about the Linsanity phenomenon, but also about the recent trade of Tim Tebow to the Jets. Both athletes were selected by *Time Magazine* as two of its Top 100 Most Influential People in the World. They were two of only six athletes named to the list and by the far the most popular in the United States. As a further testament to the respect Jeremy had in both the athletic and academic communities, he was asked to write the portion of the magazine piece on why Tebow was selected. Jeremy wrote:

Watching Tim Tebow play football, you can observe many things about his character. You see his fierce competitiveness, his strong work ethic, and how he is a leader that his teammates trust and respect.

But it is the qualities that Tim, twenty-four, embodies in his life off the field that truly set him apart. He is unashamed of his convictions and faith, and he lives a life that consistently reflects his values, day in and day out. Through his foundation, he constantly reaches out to people and communities in need of hope. He realizes what he has been blessed with and seeks to help those who are worse off. As athletes, we pour our hearts into winning games. Tim is a reminder that life is about much more than that.

The honor of writing about why Jeremy was selected went to Harvard graduate and United States Secretary of Education, Arne Duncan. Duncan wrote:

Jeremy Lin's story is a great lesson for kids everywhere because it debunks and defangs so many of the prejudices and stereotypes that unfairly hold children back. He's dispelled the idea that Asian American guards somehow couldn't hack it in the NBA—and that being a world-class athlete on the court is somehow at odds with being an excellent student off the court.

Contrary to what you might read, Jeremy, twenty-three, is no overnight sensation. In fact, he achieved success the old-fashioned way: He earned it. He worked hard and stayed humble. He lives the right way; he plays the right way.

It's great to see good values rewarded in professional sports because that's not always the case. Often it's the bling, the glam, the individual that gets celebrated—not the team and working together to advance a goal bigger than oneself. Jeremy cares only about one thing—winning. And I don't care whether you are an Asian American kid, white, black, or Hispanic. Jeremy's story tells you that if you show grit, discipline, and integrity, you too can get an opportunity to overcome the odds.

So once again, Lin and Tebow were linked. The amount of respect that Jeremy had garnered after his short time in the spotlight could be seen by the fact that he was asked to write about Tim Tebow, while the United States Secretary of Education was asked to write about Jeremy. And just to be named to the prestigious *Time Magazine* list was an honor in itself.

Back to Basketball

Traveling to Cleveland to face the Cavaliers, the Knicks received some welcomed news. Amar'e Stoudemire had been cleared to play after missing thirteen games with his back injury. You would think the team would have been sky high by getting Stoudemire back and coming off a couple of impressive wins. Instead, they were flat, and lost to a very mediocre Cavs team, 98-90. Stoudemire played well considering it was his first game back, scoring 15 points. But Anthony had just 12 and sat out the final quarter. Baron Davis sat out with a stomach virus and Jared Jeffries, who had returned to limited duty, sat out a second straight game because his right knee was again sore.

Next came the Hawks in Atlanta and the Knicks rediscovered their mojo, winning by a 113-112 count as Anthony scored 39 and Stoudemire partially blocked Marvin Williams' dunk attempt as the Hawks tried for the win. Stoudemire also contributed 22 points and the sometimes forgotten Landry Fields had 18. The team played without Tyson Chandler, who was given a night off to rest for the playoffs. It was obvious that the team missed him.

"It just shows how valuable Tyson Chandler is when he's out of the game," Coach Woodson said, afterward. "He plugs holes when there are breakdowns."

The win kept the Knicks' hold on the seventh playoff seed with slim hopes that they could move up into the sixth spot. That would be welcomed by all, since the seventh seed would likely draw the Miami Heat in the first round, and the Heat were a tough nut to crack. After the game, Jeremy provided an update on his condition via Twitter.

He wrote that he had jogged for the first time that morning and appeared to be on schedule for a return to the court six weeks after his surgery. But he added that the telling sign would be when he was able to jump and to cut. Without that ability, he would not be of much help. He knew it and the team knew it. They could only hope that maybe his schedule would accelerate and/or somehow they could get past the Heat. With two games left before the playoffs, the moment of truth would be coming soon.

There was also some off-court news before the final regular-season games. Carmelo Anthony gave Mike Woodson his full backing by saying he would love to have the interim coach be the permanent coach the next season.

"Just to see what he's brought to our team," Anthony said, "the confidence that he's installed into everybody, the belief that he has in everybody. Just his coaching style and the way he coached. Kind of a hard-nosed coach who holds everybody accountable. I've always said that. Everybody is responsible for their own actions. I would love to see him around here."

Woodson had coached the team to a 16-6 record since taking over from Mike D'Antoni and had done it while dealing with a myriad of injuries. That spoke for something and the coach admitted he wanted to come back.

"I'd love to," he said. "I think when you've been given an opportunity to start something, then you'd love to finish it."

The Knicks seemed to move in that direction when owner James Dolan removed the interim tag from General Manager Glen Grunwald and made him the permanent VP/General Manager. Grunwald and Woodson went way back, having played three seasons together in Indiana and word was that the two men got along great and were on the same page basketball-wise. When asked about Grunwald in February, Woodson had said, "He's one of the reasons I wanted to come here. You want to work with people you know."

So it appeared that the team was finally stabilizing after so many years of chaos. It's always best when the general manager and head coach are on the same page and have the owner's approval. There was already speculation about who Grunwald would bring back. If the team gave their $5 million mid-level exception to Jeremy, it might be tough to resign both Steve Novak and J. R. Smith . . . but the Knicks would wait until after the season to deal with that. There was still basketball to be played.

Before the final regular season games, there was some more Jeremy Lin news. Jeremy had gone through a light workout during the team's Wednesday morning shootaround; a workout that including jogging and shooting drills. Still being very careful, he wore a knee brace throughout the workout. It had been a little over three weeks since the April 2 surgery.

"I'd like to think if we're able to get out of this first round that he should be ready for the second round," Mike Woodson said. "But that's not for me to determine. He's got to come to us, along with the doctors, and say that the knee feels fine and he's confident that he can cut and do things that he once did. Then, we'll put him back in uniform."

While Jeremy acknowledged that he might be able to return if the team made it to the second round, he also remained the consummate team player by saying he wouldn't want his presence to mess with the team's chemistry. But he coach knew how badly he wanted to return.

"He's starting to smell the gym a little bit more now, which is great," Woodson said. "I asked him yesterday how he felt after getting out running a little bit, and he said he felt pretty good. But we've got to put him through drills where he's cutting and things of that nature just to make sure that the knee doesn't swell up and he's not physically sore. I mean, there's going to be some soreness, but we've got to make sure that when he steps back out on the floor, he's able to play basketball."

Jeremy, of course, was smart enough not to push it. He wasn't about to risk a more serious injury nor would he play if he didn't feel he could really help the team. So the wait would continue and the Knicks would have to try to beat the Heat without him. That matchup was all but confirmed after the Knicks beat the Clippers, 99-93, with a balanced team effort. An Orlando win over Charlotte eliminated any chance of New York moving up to the sixth seed. All the Knicks had to do was beat Charlotte in the regular season finale and it would be set-up a matchup with the Heat.

And that's just what happened. New York easily beat the hapless Bobcats, 104-84, despite holding Anthony, Chandler, and Davis out of the lineup. J. R. Smith had 22 points while

Stoudemire scored 21 in just a little over a half. Then the bench took over. Little used rookie Josh Harrellson had 18 points and veteran Mike Bibby handed out 12 assists. The team finished the abbreviated, post-lockout schedule with a 36-30 mark. Not bad, considering all that had transpired in an up-and-down season.

One final note before the playoffs began. The NBA released its most popular jersey list for the season. Chicago's Derrick Rose had the largest selling jersey, but right behind him was Jeremy Lin, selling more jerseys than the likes of Kobe Bryant, LeBron James, Carmelo Anthony, and Dwayne Wade, who followed him on the list.

Jeremy, of course, had come from nowhere; but once Linsanity took off, it never stopped. As one observer put it, "Lin wasn't just an on-court success, he brought real, tangible financial benefits to the league and the Knicks."

The bottom line generated by Jeremy made everyone happy, but he himself would probably have traded in all those jerseys for two healthy knees and the ability to play the entire season. But what's done is done. Everyone, including Jeremy, was ready to move forward.

Chapter Eleven: The Playoffs and Beyond

THE AFTERNOON BEFORE the Knicks took the court to face the Heat in Game 1 in Miami, Jeremy Lin was playing one-on-one on the American Airlines Arena court. He was running, doing some cutting, and moving laterally, working against assistant coach Kenny Atkinson, which some saw as an indication that he was ahead of schedule in his rehab. Could he return sometime during the first round?

There was no official change in the six-week prognosis, though team doctors wanted to see how Jeremy's knee responded to the workout before deciding whether it was feasible for him to return earlier than expected. Of course, he'd still need time to get into game shape, which doesn't happen overnight. From the time Jeremy saw his first extended playing time against the Nets, through the period of Linsanity, and then playing for Mike Woodson before the injury, Jeremy had averaged 18.5 points and 7.6 assists in twenty-six games, twenty-five of them as the starter. That's what the Knicks would be missing from the point as they got ready to face the Heat. Baron Davis would be the starter with veteran Mike Bibby as his backup.

If the Knicks had any hope of winning the series and then getting Jeremy back for the second round, the Heat pretty much took care of that in the opener, destroying New York by an embarrassing, 100-67, tally. Tyson Chandler, hampered by the flu, was totally ineffective, Anthony had a bad game, and then to add insult to injury, rookie Iman Shumpert, a key to the team's defense, went down with what appeared to be a serious, season-ending knee injury. The team suspected he had torn his ACL, an injury that required reconstructive knee surgery.

The Knicks managed to hold it together for about a quarter and a half. When J. R. Smith and Steve Novak hit long three-pointers, the Knickerbockers pulled to a 30-29 lead with 6:53 left in the half. That's when the roof fell in. Miami outscored the Knicks 24-2, and had broken it open with a halftime score of 54-31. James, Wade, Bosh, and company just cruised from there. The game was rough and sometimes chippy, with several players jawing at each other. But there was no avoiding that final score.

There wasn't much good news coming out of the game. Shumpert indeed had torn his ACL and would have to deal with rehab before returning next season. Baron Davis had a solid, 10-point first quarter, but then said his back was acting up and he shut it down for the final twenty-one minutes. Anthony had hit just 3 of 15 shots and Stoudemire was 2 of 7. The Knicks had now lost eleven consecutive playoff games dating back to 2001, the second longest such streak in NBA history. Could things get any worse?

With the season looking as if it was going to end quickly, there was perhaps one ray of hope. Could a sudden burst of

Linsanity save the day? The day after his one-on-one workout, Jeremy told the media that he was still hoping to rejoin the injury-plagued Knicks before the first round was over. He said he was picking up the pace of his rehab and was motivated by the terrible outing he had against the Heat the last time he faced them before being hurt.

"My last game against Miami, I was one for eleven with a bunch of turnovers," he said. "That's obviously in my mind, too. I don't want that to be my last game."

But could he get back during the first round? "I don't really want to make a promise," he said, "because I just don't know. If I felt good today, then that would be more of a possibility. But I don't feel that great today."

Jeremy explained that he was able to do a lot more than he expected a day earlier, but now was feeling some of the aftereffects of that first real workout. "It was just two days ago that I started running," he explained. It happened really fast. But today I took a step back. We'll have to see. When I come back I want to create energy and be aggressive."

A day later there was more talk about Game 4, which would be at Madison Square Garden the following Sunday.

"I'm going to evaluate at the end of the week and see how I feel," he said. "Hopefully I'll feel good. Every time I come into the gym, the playoff atmosphere is unbelievable. I want to feel it and want to help my teammates."

It was apparent that Jeremy was itching to come back and wanted to experience the playoffs, which present a decidedly more intense atmosphere than most games in the regular season. But he said again that he didn't want to make himself "vulnerable to something more serious," then adding, "I think when I can take a hit and when I can cut at full speed and not think about it, I'll be ready."

As much as he wanted Jeremy back, Coach Woodson wasn't counting his chickens. "He was out shooting," the coach said. "He went through some of our scripted offense, which was nice to see. But again, he's day to day. I don't know when he's coming back."

While the speculation about Jeremy continued and fans kept their fingers crossed, the Knicks and Heat took to the court for Game 2. This one wasn't a blowout, but had its own drama; something that added to the roller-coaster, soap-opera type Knicks' season. The Heat won the game, 104-94, giving the Knicks an ignominious NBA record of twelve straight playoff losses. Without Iman Shumpert's defense, Dwayne Wade had 25 points, while Chris Bosh had 21 and LeBron James contributed 19. The so-called "Big Three" had done their job, negating a 30-point effort from Anthony.

But the real drama came moments after the game ended. Amar'e Stoudemire, who played a decent game with 18 points and seven rebounds, was so frustrated by the loss that he punched a glass-enclosed fire extinguisher in the hallway leading to the locker room. The force of the blow shattered the glass, and within seconds, there was blood everywhere. Stoudemire received numerous stitches in his left hand, which the team described as "lacerated," and suddenly his status for Game 3, as well as the remainder of the playoffs, was in doubt. It may have been a spur-of-the-moment reaction, but it was a needless injury at the worst possible time.

"I saw a lot of blood," said one of the Knicks. "I'm squeamish, so I got out of there. He punched it (the glass). I don't know if it was open hand or not."

"Your emotions run high," Tyson Chandler said. "In a split second, a decision can alter things. You can't fault anybody. We've got to deal with the repercussions."

Carmelo Anthony seemed to wonder if the team was jinxed. "It's a tough situation," he said. "It seems like it's always something happening—snakebit. [Amar'e] is one of the keys on this team. I need him fighting with me."

Stoudemire left the arena with his left arm in a sling and didn't speak with reporters. Later he communicated via Twitter.

"I am so mad at myself right now," he tweeted. "I want to apologize to the fans and my team, not proud of my actions, headed home for a new start."

The team had certainly been decimated. Shumpert joined Lin on the sidelines with a knee injury. Davis was still playing with a balky back and Chandler was trying to shake off the affects of the flu. Now Stoudemire could be done.

The next day it was reported that Stoudemire had some minor hand surgery to repair a small muscle and the word was that he probably would be out for at least the Heat series. Witnesses said he had punched the glass while walking quickly past the fire extinguisher and the motion allowed the glass fragments to rip the side of his hand. Someone mentioned that the death of his brother in an auto accident earlier in the season had continued to affect Stoudemire, and his continuing grief might have contributed to his actions. He was officially declared out for Game 3 and doubtful for Sunday's Game 4.

That wasn't the last of the Knicks' news. Jeremy had participated in a three-on-three scrimmage on Wednesday, and said he
would sit down with Coach Woodson to discuss the possibility
of him playing in Sunday's Game 4.

"This is the first time he's been able to run up and down,"
Woodson said. "He's gone through a lot of drills. The rest will
come if he can cut and guard people and be able to handle the
play and makes plays off the dribble. I'll sit down with him
[later] along with the doctors and see how he feels from running up and down in this stretch."

The next day's news was not good. Jeremy pretty much ruled
out playing in Game 4, saying the knee was still too sore after
going through the contact scrimmage the day before. Game 5
was a possibility, but he said for that to happen he'd have to
show dramatic improvement.

"I don't want to say I am or am not," he explained. "Game 4
doesn't look great. Game 5, I have no idea. I'll see how quickly
I can get to the point where I can trust it and not think about
it and get my full explosiveness, cut and more importantly,
defensively being able to move laterally."

He said he would continue to scrimmage between Games 3
and 4.

"It depends on how the knee reacts to everyday things," Jeremy
said. "We're going to add more, trying to jump and finish and see
how it reacts. It's tough to really put a date on it. Today was the day
after my first day of contact. It wasn't the best. It wasn't the worst."

If some fans were hoping for a Linsanity miracle, it now
appeared that wouldn't happen. The second round? The odds
against a second round happening were not good, especially

with the additional injuries to Shumpert and Stoudemire. All the Knicks could do was soldier on.

With the series returning to the Garden, Knicks' fans were hoping to see at least one victory; a small thing to ask, rather just something to end the playoff drought and give them hope for the next season. But with three starters out (Lin, Shumpert, and Stoudemire), the task seemed almost hopeless. Even Carmelo Anthony wondered if the team could score enough points to win. Coach Woodson said he would move Anthony into Stoudemire's spot at power forward and hope for the best.

"I don't think Miami's gonna let me beat them by myself," Anthony said. "Everybody's got to do it. Everybody's got to step up."

Try as they might and encouraged by a loud crowd, the Knicks fought hard, trailing by just a 58-56 count going into the fourth quarter. But like previous match-ups, they again disappeared offensively as the Heat pulled away for an 87-70 victory and what looked like an insurmountable 3-0 lead in the series. Anthony, in trying to do too much, came up small with a 7 for 23 shooting performance and just 22 points.

"Offensively, we just didn't have it," said Woodson, afterward. "We were stagnant. I have to take the blame for it."

But the real blame had to be the injuries. Sure, great teams can overcome them, but that maxim holds more for sports like baseball and football. Lose a key player or two in basketball and it's hard to make up the difference. It also happened to the top-seeded Bulls (who were tied with the Spurs for the best record in the league) when they lost star point guard Derrick Rose to an ACL tear and subsequently lost their opening series to the Sixers, the eighth seed (who had the worst record of any team to make the playoffs). But the Knicks weren't about to use that as an excuse. It was a just fact of life. The team was woefully undermanned. They also learned again that they wouldn't be getting any help from Jeremy in Game 4.

"I haven't been able to load it or jump or explode or drive by somebody the way I want to, so it's going to be longer than that," he said. "I just want to take it day by day."

But the Knicks did get a boost before Game 5. Amar'e Stoudemire declared himself ready to play in a move that surprised everyone. Not only did he play, but he played well. And with a resurgent Anthony scoring 41 points and Stoudemire adding 20 and 10 rebounds, the Knicks surprised everyone, including the Heat, and took an 89-87 victory, ending their winless playoff streak and sending the series back to Miami.

Stoudemire called it "a last-minute decision" to play with a heavily bandaged left hand. "It doesn't feel great," he said. "What makes it feel much better is we won."

But what would a Knicks game be without another injury . . . and this was a bad one. Baron Davis crumpled to the court with 5:15 left in the third quarter as he tried to lead a fast-break and had to be carried off on a stretcher. The immediate diagnosis was a dislocated kneecap, a bad enough injury to be considered career-ending. Later, it was found he had done even more damage. In essence, he had wrecked the knee. At his age, it's doubtful if he'd ever play again.

So with Game 5 looming, thoughts again turned to Lin. Would he or wouldn't he? It was becoming almost a daily game, and the lyrics of the song were beginning to sound the same.

"He'll get back in the gym [today] and talk to doctors about where he is physically," said Woodson. "Then we'll make some decisions before we get on the plane to head to Miami."

Carmelo Anthony wasn't sure either, but he did give the injured point guard an endorsement. "Jeremy is still part of this team," he said. "He's injured right now, but he's still part of this team. I look forward to having him back next season."

But what about this season?

The Final Countdown

The day before Game 5, Mike Woodson told the media he's "not counting" on Jeremy being in the lineup, despite the crying need for a point guard. Instead, veteran Mike Bibby would get the start.

"We'll gauge it, but I'm not counting on Jeremy Lin to play," Woodson explained. "So we've just got to continue where we've been with the guys in uniform. I'm not counting on him to play."

Though Jeremy was now scrimmaging, there was a huge difference between that and the intensity of playoff basketball, as Woodson further explained. "He's not in great shape. Playoff basketball, you have to be at an all-time high, and he hasn't played in a while. I don't know if that will be a determining factor with the doctors."

Finally, after Tuesday's practice, the coach made it definite, telling the press that Jeremy would not only miss Game 5, but wouldn't be available if, by some miracle, the series continued.

"He's just not ready," the coach said. "[The doctors] will let him know when he's ready and I'm sure he'll step up to the plate and say he's ready when that time comes. Right now he's not. He's not physically ready to play."

Even Carmelo Anthony, who wanted to win as much as anyone, felt that it was too risky for Jeremy to force himself to play. Said Anthony, "I talked to Jeremy. We had a private conversation about it. What we talked about, I'll keep it between ourselves. My main thing is him just being healthy. If he's not 100 percent healthy, there's no need to come out here no matter how many minutes he'll play. He hasn't been playing. I want him to take care of himself."

On the Wednesday morning before Game 5, Jeremy finally addressed the situation and his concerns about forcing the issue and coming back too soon.

"I'm mostly worried about just not having to suffer a real setback, which would be a new knee injury," he said, adding there was still pain and soreness in the knee after his workouts. "There was nothing to set it back. I think to get from 85 percent to 100 percent takes more time than I may have thought."

Jeremy also said that the doctors had cautioned him about returning too soon. "They said I need to be able to just trust the knee and right now there's some tightness and soreness, and I need to get that out before I can be 100 percent," he explained. "That's what we're doing, a lot of manual stuff, get everything out, all the stuff that doesn't need to be there . . . just trying to make it pain free."

As is usually the case, there were some who questioned Jeremy, invoking the old adage of a guy toughing it out for the sake of the team. Why not suit up and at least give the team five or ten minutes? Some even questioned the Knicks, saying they didn't want to risk a guy whose popularity continued to bring in millions in merchandise sales. But what probably caused the questions was the constant back and forth; the maybe next game, maybe next game. At first it sounded as if Jeremy's rehab was ahead of schedule. Now it was beginning to sound as if it was behind. Why were they dangling a carrot? Perhaps they didn't want to have the fans give up on the season . . . or on Jeremy.

In reality, this is what happens when an athlete is rehabbing an injury. There are good days and bad days. Jeremy would be a free agent after the season, and while he already expressed a preference to return to the Knicks, nothing was set in stone. If he played and re-injured his knee or needed additional surgery, his career could very well hang in the balance. Again, he tried to explain.

"What was it, like two days ago, I tried to take off, tried to plant, just to go full speed at 100 percent. It just didn't feel right. I felt pain when I tried to take off. I thought it would go away over time, in terms of timetables. When I worked out I was probably going 80, 85 percent and I just figured in a week I might be 100. There was nothing to set it back. But it just didn't happen. Like I said, getting from 85 percent to 100 takes more time than I may have thought."

No one can get inside an athletes' knee, shoulder, elbow, ankle, hip, or wherever he's hurt. Most professional athletes know their bodies well; know when they feel right and are ready to go. Apparently, Jeremy didn't have the sense that he was ready. And when he explained his symptoms to his doctors, they obviously advised him not to play. That was the bottom line. He just wasn't ready. And to be honest, it wasn't like the

Knicks were a Jeremy Lin away from winning the NBA title. How much, at this point, could he really help?

So the Knicks went into Game 5 undermanned and shredded by injuries. That's no way to face LeBron James and his cohorts; and to the surprise of no one, Miami closed them out, 106-94, showing more firepower and more athleticism than the Knickerbockers, a team now without a championship for a thirty-ninth straight season. Anthony scored 35 points in his final game. But it was Tyson Chandler who tasted an NBA title the season before with Dallas that expressed the disappointment most felt.

"I'm personally very disappointed. This is unacceptable to me," he said. "I didn't come here to lose in the first round, and I don't plan on doing this in the future. I'll do everything I can to make this team better in the future."

As for Coach Woodson, he tried to make the best of the situation while hoping he would get a chance to return and finish the job.

"I'm so happy for our ballclub," he said. "They fought all year to get to this point. [But] I don't want them to be satisfied because the ultimate goal is to win an NBA title."

. . .

As soon as the final buzzer sounded, the postseason work and the questions would begin. Would Woodson become the permanent head coach? Would Jeremy Lin be back? How about Steve Novak and/or J. R. Smith? Did the team feel Stoudemire could work with Anthony, or would they trade him? How would Iman Shumpert recover from major knee surgery? By all indications, management was leaning toward retaining Woodson. And they seemed to want Lin, though some felt they would also look to sign a veteran point guard to share time with him as he learned.

As for Jeremy, he definitely sounded as if he wanted to return, though he also knew the realities of the business. And while he thrived under Mike D'Antoni's system, he also seemed to enjoy playing for Mike Woodson. "I think he's gotten a lot out of all the players, the way we finished the season, the way we were playing defense," Jeremy said of his coach. "We were the number one defensive team during one stretch. I think he's done a great job with this team and how he uses the players and what he gets out of the players. It's a nice mix in terms of putting people in spots they need to be in and also spacing the floor and having the creativity."

As for returning, he said, "I don't really want to guess. You never know what happens in this business. Nobody really knows what's going to happen. I'm definitely comfortable here. I love playing in New York. I love the fans. They gave me the chance. They believed in me. That why I'm here today. I owe a lot to this organization."

It sounded like a mutual admiration society between player and coach. Mike Woodson, who was skeptical about Jeremy when he first took over the team, now seemed to genuinely want the young guard back.

Jeremy's a big part of our team. Will he start? Only time will tell. He has to recover from his knee and use the summer to work on his game to put himself in the best position for our ballclub. He has started for our team and he has played well for our basketball team. But this summer will be very pivotal for him in terms of his improvement, and the future is very bright for him. There's still room for growth. He's still gotta learn the NBA game and what it's about playing at a high level. There's no doubt in my mind that he's a smart enough player that he will get better in time, but he needs the reps just like all young players. It doesn't happen overnight. Will he be back next year? Absolutely. He's a big part of our ballclub.

Spoken like a veteran coach who leans toward veteran players. It sounded like Woodson certainly wanted him back, but would also like they needed a savvy veteran to mentor him, maybe someone like free agent Steve Nash. But that was only part of the Knicks off-season equation. Many still pointed to Carmelo Anthony as the key. There was little doubt that Melo was one of the NBA's best scorers, but his style often resulted in slowing the offense while he worked his way for a shot. Anthony would still be the top scorer on a well-blended offense, but the shots would also be there for others. It would be up to Woodson, assuming he was retained as coach, to create this situation and persuade Anthony to function within it.

There was little doubt that the Knicks had improved defensively under Woodson and that the players seemed to like the results. Pushed by a strong coach and the defensive presence of Tyson Chandler, the team's defense should continue to improve.

In mid-May, the NBA Players Association filed for an arbitration hearing with the league. They were fighting a loophole in the new collective bargaining agreement that would give the Knicks more flexibility to re-sign Lin while keeping their $5 million mid-level exception and use it to sign a veteran point guard. Basically, they were saying that players claimed off waivers, as was the case with Lin and Novak, should be looked upon the same way as a player who was traded. It would enable them to keep their "Bird rights," which are exceptions that allow teams to exceed the salary cap to re-sign their own players. If they were successful, it would give the team more flexibility.

While awaiting the ruling, Jeremy got some good news. He was named to the U.S. Select Team that will scrimmage against the U.S. Olympic Team in Las Vegas in July as the team prepares for the upcoming London Games. That will give Jeremy some valuable game experience before training camp begins. In the meantime, the jockeying and the talk continued. Jeremy's agent, Roger Montgomery, was telling people that nothing was assured as far as Jeremy's future with the Knicks. He was due to officially become a free agent on July 1.

Montgomery said he didn't expect an easy negotiation. "No, I don't expect that," he said. "We're not anticipating that's going to happen. We don't have assurances of anything. I know history shows most restricted free agents go back to their team, but I'm not going to assume anything. We're waiting to see what happens."

The cautious words of a good agent. Assume nothing. But it was difficult to see Jeremy not returning. For starters, he proved in a short time to be a very good NBA basketball player. A marginal player simply could not have accomplished the things Jeremy did during the first onset of Linsanity. He showed himself to be tough and fearless, had an instinctual sense for the game, and didn't wilt during crunch time. It seemed logical that he would only get better. Then you add the intangibles, especially his popularity not only in New York, but around the league, and it made very little sense for the Knicks to lose a player who also kept the cash register ringing.

The next piece of offseason business involved the coach. In the last week of May, the Knicks made what everyone expected official. Mike Woodson was given a three-year contract extension, which eliminated the "interim" and made him their full-time head coach. For once, owner James Dolan didn't go after a high-priced big name, such as Phil Jackson, but stuck with the guy who had solidified the team and brought them into the playoffs.

"Mike took over the team under challenging circumstances and made it clear, starting on Day One, that he was going to hold every player on our roster accountable," Dolan said in a statement. "We saw a significant improvement since Mike took over and believe our team will only keep improving under Mike's direction."

General Manager Glen Grunwald added, "We told Woody he would get the first crack at the job, and he hit it out of the park."

The next day, Grunwald spoke again, this time talking about Jeremy Lin, once again indicating that the team wanted him back.

"We can keep him if we want him," Grunwald said, "and we do want to keep him. And I believe Jeremy has had a great experience here and I believe he wants to come back."

The Knicks, apparently, were waiting for the arbitration ruling on the Bird rights to see what kind of maneuverability they had, not only with regard to Jeremy, but to Steve Novak as well; and perhaps even to gauge their chances of signing a veteran point guard. So the official news on Jeremy would probably have to wait a bit longer. The hearing on the restoring the Bird rights was tentatively set for June 13.

Another piece of Jeremy news also broke about the same time. The United States Patent and Trademark Office had rejected the remaining applicants trying to cash in on the Linsanity trademark. Jeremy, through his attorney, has officially applied for the trademark on February 13. Nearly a dozen other applicants continued to try to get permission to use the name until this final ruling came down. And, apparently, the trademark office was also working to prevent spins off the name or phonetic version, such as "Lynn." Though Jeremy certainly didn't come close to the profile of a greedy athlete, he was certainly within his rights to trademark the well-known variation of his name. After all, he created Linsanity with his exceptional play. If anyone was going to control it, it should be him.

As the free agency season approached, the Knicks received some good news. The Players Association were successful in their fight for the Bird rights. The door was now open for the Knicks to sign both Jeremy and Steve Novak, if they wished, and still have room to acquire a veteran point guard. In late June, Jeremy withdrew from the Olympic Select Team because he still hadn't signed with a team. He would also test the free agent waters. If another team were to offer him a contract, the Knicks had the right to match it and still sign him. That seemed to be their intent, and the wait began.

· · ·

Jeremy Lin's story is far from over . . . on the contrary, it is really just beginning, and in a way few sports stories have before. His rise from a guy at the end of the bench to a player the whole country was watching sounds almost like a fairy tale. But Jeremy is no comic-book hero. He didn't don a cape or magical suit and suddenly become a star. He was a guy who bucked the odds through hard work and perseverance, stayed mentally strong, and waited for the chance that almost didn't come.

Along the way he had to overcome several negative stereotypes that said there were long odds of him becoming an NBA player, much less a good one. How many Ivy League graduates made it to the NBA? And how many Asian Americans had the physical attributes to complete in an increasingly physically demanding league? He sat at the end of the bench for three teams in a little more than one full season, made several trips to the D-League, and by all accounts, was just about ready to be phased out for a third time when a confluence of circumstances gave him a chance. That's when his story took an abrupt turn.

Not only did Jeremy make the most of the opportunity when Mike D'Antoni gave him his chance, but he also became one of those special athletes who seemed to draw fans from all walks of life. Once he began leading the injury-riddled Knicks to one victory after another, the term Linsanity was born, and it was one of those magical nicknames that just connected. Boom. Just like that, Jeremy Lin was an overnight phenomenon. He became not only an inspiration to Asian Americans, but to underdogs everywhere. And his popularity crossed oceans as he drew millions of fans in all the Asian countries, especially in Taiwan and China. His jersey and other merchandise began flying off the shelves, and he was suddenly the most popular and sought-after player in a star-studded NBA.

Though he began his Knickerbocker run in a system that was perfectly suited to him, a coaching change forced him to change, and he was adapting to Mike Woodson's coaching style very well when a knee injury stopped him in his tracks. By that time, he had won over Woodson by virtue of his pure toughness and ability to raise his game in the fourth quarter, especially at crunch time. Injuries, of course, are one of those X-factors in sports, and because of it, Jeremy's season ended as quickly as it began.

But his story is far from over. The combination of the shortened season, his time on the bench early, and then a knee injury limited Jeremy to just 35 games as a New York Knick in the 2011–2012 season. Yet he averaged 14.6 points a game, 6.2 assists, 1.6 steals, and 3.1 rebounds. And that included the nine games in which he played sparingly before his breakthrough game against the Nets. Those numbers certainly reflect talent. Coach Woodson is right in that Jeremy still needs more game experience and perhaps he will benefit now that the Knicks have brought in veteran point guard Jason Kidd to mentor and share duties with him.

In the meantime, Jeremy's popularity should remain high. Of course, he'll have to continue to play well, but the combination of what he has already done, coupled with his desire to improve and will to win—and his strong sense of team first—should make him a first-class player. Add all that to Linsanity, plus his worldwide popularity, and the foundation for a first class NBA career is all there before him. The rest is up to Jeremy.

. . .

WHILE THE REST might be up to Jeremy, no one expected the sudden turn of events that took place in July. As a free agent, Jeremy had the right to shop his talents to any team. If he received an offer, the Knicks would have three days to match it. The organization stated publicly that it would, indeed, match any offer. Sure enough, the Houston Rockets (who released Jeremy before the start of the season) stepped forward with a $19.5 million, three-year deal, with $9.3 million to be paid the third year. By all indications, the Knicks were going to match. Knowing this, the Rockets suddenly upped the offer to include a $14.9 million payout for the third year. If the Knicks matched, it would put them over the luxury tax threshold that year and could wind up costing them $35 million or more. It would result in them paying just four players—Anthony, Stoudemire, Chandler, and Lin—a total of $76.4 million for the 2014–15 season.

As popular as Jeremy was in New York, the Knicks were not happy and felt like Jeremy was dealing behind their backs. They went out and agreed to a sign-and-trade with the Portland Trail Blazers, in which they would trade defensive specialist Jared Jeffries and reserve center Dan Gadzuric for veteran center Kurt Thomas (who spent seven years with the Knicks, from 1998–2005) and point guard Raymond Felton, who had his best season as a Knick under Mike D'Antoni (but was traded away in the Carmelo Anthony deal). With future hall-of-fame point guard Jason Kidd also signed, it began to look as if the Knicks wouldn't match Houston's offer after all. Despite a fan protest, in which over 14,000 people signed a petition to keep him, that's just what happened.

At the July 17 deadline, the Knicks announced they were cutting ties with Jeremy and Linsanity. He would officially be going to the Houston Rockets. Though Jeremy was within his rights to do what he did with Houston, the Knicks were within their rights to refuse to match. Once the news came, Jeremy quickly tweeted:

> Much love and thankfulness to the Knicks and New York for your support this past year...easily the best year of my life #ForeverGrateful

· · ·

So LINSANITY WILL be moving on. Jeremy will have to prove himself in Houston, where he will quickly find a new legion of fans (who quickly embraced Yao Ming, the 7'6" center who played his entire career in Houston after being drafted by the team in 2002), while continuing to have the support of Asian Americans all over the country.

With all that's happened since his breakout game in New Jersey, it'll still be up to Jeremy Lin to show that he's the real deal—the guy who led the Knicks on that incredible winning streak that captured the fancy of sports fans across the globe.